BEYOND SELF DOUBT

JOURNEY OF A SOUTHERN BLACK WOMAN

Delilah Yvonne Marrow

SoAllMayKnow
PUBLISHING

BEYOND SELF DOUBT
Published by So All May Know Publishing
P O Box 6718
Largo, MD 20792

soallmayknow@gmail.com
www.carethacrawford.com

SoAllMayKnow
PUBLISHING

© 2019 by Delilah Yvonne Marrow

Cover design by Caretha Franks Crawford

Printed in the United States of America

ISBN 978-0-578-56750-1

To Laurie, Thanks for [handwritten signature] Delilah Yvonne Marrow November 2019

DEDICATION TO MY FAMILY

To my children, grandchildren, great-grandchildren, and all of the generations that come after I am no longer here in the flesh:

I have written these few highlights of my journey to shine a little light on just who I am. If you were privileged to know me while you could still see, touch, or hear my laughter, then you will have a memory or two that will bring me into your presence. When you share these memories with each other, family members or with people who did not know me, you keep me alive. That is why my motto is to live forever.

I traveled a remarkable journey. I got to walk through doors that were opened for me, and experience some pretty amazing happenings. I got to open a few doors for others, which made my heart glad. I got to see and experience other parts of the world and share with people from different cultures. I was confronted with many challenges that took courage and fortitude to overcome. I asked for help when it was very difficult to do so. I sustained a few health challenges. Thank God for healthcare professionals, and a caring family

My advice to you is always put forward the best in yourself, and you will see the best in others. Remember we are all created in God's image, and God loves every one of us. The whole world is ours to explore. "Live each day to the fullest. Take advantage of every moment and every hour. Be your best self, and always look for the best in others."

Love,
Mom, Nana, Grandma?

PREFACE

by Yvette, Karen & Greta

It is a privilege and an honor to share our mother with you. As small children, we did not realize how blessed we were to have Delilah Yvonne Wooten Marrow as our mother...she was just "mommy."

She is also affectionately known as momma, nana, sister, aunt, cousin, friend, mentor, scholar and teacher among other terms of endearment.

She is truly the "Butterfly" that she considers as the metaphoric symbol of herself. However, that moniker, "the butterfly," is only a fragment of who she is to us. She is a blessing, God's gift, and a remarkable woman.

As she emerges from her cocoon, you will join her as she reveals her story of struggle and triumph. You will read about an astounding woman who has lived a full and fulfilling life. The challenges she faced as well as the doors she opened have provided a roadmap for life. She has inspired us to be independent, and unapologetic when contemplating making tough decisions in life. The platform of a" butterfly" lites on the flower for just a moment in time before it flies off to explore something new. Mom has been strategically perched in many places of our lives (floating above and beside us), showing us a path of grace and beauty. Fascinating in countless ways, her journey is infused with ever-evolving life transformations that are not your typical unwrapping of layers of an onion; rather, the unfolding and blossoming of a beautiful butterfly. Her newly developed wings gave her the ability to soar to new heights as she experienced the wonderment of life.

You will accompany her on a journey full of emotions, adventure, innovation, encouragement, and spiritual enlightenment—to name a few. She still leads and nurtures by example; demonstrating how to persevere through the toughest times and rejoice in times of gladness. We are so fortunate to be still able to glean these pearls of wisdom from a woman who has seen and done so much for herself and others. She displays genuine compassion and empathy toward others, especially those less fortunate.

Through her eyes, you will discover her outstanding accomplishments and achievements as she undergoes an awakening and rebirth. You will be filled with excitement, feel her pain, marvel at her inspiration and dedication to her faith and the church, her devotion, and commitment to her family, and her selfless acts of kindness to absolutely everyone she encounters. Moreover, as many of you are aware, our mother leaves an indelible impression with everyone she comes in contact with, and everywhere she goes.....and she gets around. She made a point of physically "being there" for so very many family members to either participate and/or support them regardless of age or occasion, whether domestically or internationally. As an avid traveler, she is also known as the most moving family member of the Wooten family with 20+ relocations. She purposely moved closer to all three of us to spend quality time with each of us. And now she happily resides with Greta's family.

What our mother has contributed to her family, friends, church, and more is limitless and will be utilized indefinitely for generations to come. Just like the handprints on the legendary Walk of Fame at Grauman's Chinese Theater, "her mark" will forever be imprinted on them. Thanks be to God for Delilah Yvonne Wooten Marrow!

Who Can Find A Virtuous Woman?
Proverbs 31:10, 25-31

"His lord said unto him, Well done, thou good and faithful servant: thou hast been faithful over a few things, I will make thee ruler over many things: enter thou into the joy of thy lord."
Matthew 25:21 (KJV)

Karen, Greta & Yvette

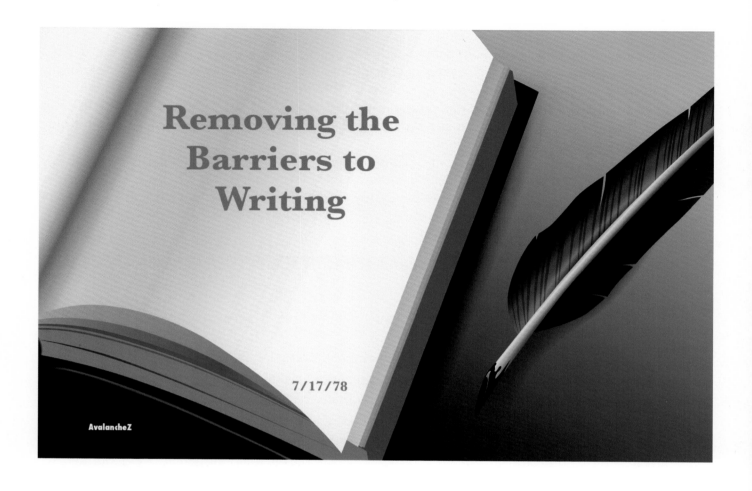

Writing has been one of the most challenging goals I have ever attempted to accomplish. Letting people know of my pain has been hard, but I have begun to share through this collection of stories, poems, prayers, love words, and reflections on my life.

Writing my story has been both painful and enlightening. Retracing the path of my journey has been revealing. I have a much clearer understanding of myself, and a greater appreciation for my parents and other ancestors.

Much of this writing was done during the decades of the 70's, and 80's when I was becoming aware of how racism and sexism had impacted my life, and my struggle to overcome the fear of showing my real strength.

I adopted the butterfly as my symbol because it represents freedom, light, tough, always on the move, and because I can identify with its stages of development.

I am especially grateful to my family, my friends, and my church for their encouragement and constant support.

Anything is possible. Even removing the barriers of writing. Maintaining rational behavior takes commitment and perseverance.

I have not documented the many workshops, and self-help programs I have participated in over the years, but there are many to help me move beyond the negativism that surface when I begin to write. Two of the most helpful organizations are 1. Toastmasters (an organization where participants write speeches and present them in front of other members of the group. The group gives immediate feedback on how well you have done or how you could improve.), and 2. Re-Evaluation Counseling-RC (an organization whose motto is that "all people are good, and we have genius size intelligence")

Leaders and other participants help individuals learn how to appreciate themselves. The primary goal of the organization is to help participants live in present time—creating a brand-new response for each unique situation.) At one of the annual workshops of RC, I made a commitment to myself, leaders of the workshop, and other participants that I would remove the barriers of writing that had kept me stuck for so many years. I committed myself to write every day and send the first draft (without correction) to two people. It was not easy to make that decision because one of the people was Harvey Jackins, the founder of Re-Evaluation Counseling, and the other was Joyce Duncan, the editor of Black Re-Emergence, the journal focused on issues written by and for Black people. These two people were very caring people, and I knew they would appreciate my words.

I began to write every day when I returned home. Since then, I have written about my experiences, and I have written lots of poetry. This has been a very revealing experience. First of all, when I read the work I have done, it is well thought about, and well structured. I have no need to be ashamed of what I write.

Secondly, I discovered part of the reason for my fear at the office is the bureaucracy. The office is structured to create anxiety. Almost everyone writes for someone else's signature. Right away, you are set up to receive negative feedback. If you submit your best thinking in a letter, memo or other written document and your thoughts happen to be different than the person who must review or sign, your best thinking may be tossed aside, and you are left feeling inadequate. You are directed to re-write until you are successful at nearly guessing the thought of the person who will review and/or sign the document.

Since I have been writing every day, I can now see clearly how this process has caused me to have negative feelings about my writing.

Another area that is very clear to me now is my need for perfection. Being a perfectionist causes anxiety. I have learned other techniques about writing that I never used effectively before. Making notes has become a viable tool for me. My whole outlook about writing has changed. Things that I knew in a theoretical sense at one time are now practical. My advice to others who might have anxieties about writing is, "just do it." It only hurts for a little while.

Delilah Yvonne, the Early Years

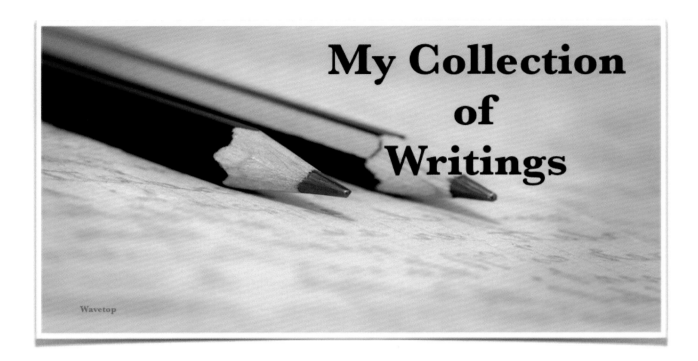

My Collection of Writings

Wavetop

The collection of writings you are about to read can be described in one or more of the following metaphors. I think of my life as a stream. A stream ebbs and flows, but continues to move. It may pick up leaves and twigs along the way, but as it moves over rocks and around boulders, the "trash" gets pushed away, and the stream continues clear and fresh. It may encounter other challenges, but it finds a way to meet the problem and continues to move.

Sometimes I think of my life experiences like a patchwork quilt. Many, many scraps of fabric in a variety of colors and shapes are used--sometimes plain or with flowers, even stripes, and dots. These pieces are sewn together to make a beautiful project that can be a gift, a hanging or used for warmth on a bed. If the pieces do not match the way you want the first try, then you must take them apart and begin again until you have just the right combination you are hoping for. That is also the way life is. "If at first, you do not succeed, try, try again."

Another metaphor is a jigsaw puzzle where there are a variety of shapes and colors that sometimes look as if they could never fit together, but as each piece is turned over and colors and shape begin to match, they form a complete picture. Some puzzles are easy to figure out, while others can take many, many hours, even days. But I do not give up, because I want to see the finished product. Life is not always easy. Life is full of many challenges to help guide us in the direction we want to go.

So, read this collection of writings not as a fixed pattern, but as a series of experiences and learnings that helped to shape who I am.

You will read about my travels. I have been a very mobile person. I traveled for pleasure, for my church, and many other reasons. I was a military spouse so moving about every three years became a part of my routine. I continued that pattern of relocating my residence many times up and down the East Coast from North Carolina to Washington, DC, to Maryland, Pennsylvania, and New Jersey for several years. I have made that complete circle a couple of times, and am now stationary in New Jersey.

Another way I enrich my life is through celebrations and hobbies. Birthday celebrations are a big thing for me. I have enjoyed many BIG milestone celebrations. You will read about things I do to keep my mind and body agile--quilting, crocheting, and table games, especially cards. I will stop almost anything to play a game of pinochle or bid whist. Or you name it, I am "game."

My mobility has allowed me to meet, and get to know a lot of people who have enriched my life, and helped me grow and overcome my struggles with writing and low self-esteem by inviting me to participate in meaningful projects and encouraging me to be a part of life-changing opportunities. There are those who validated my visions and supported me when I was "in over my head" so to speak. I excelled in spite of myself. I was no stranger to opening doors and raising awareness for others. I fought for justice and equality for all especially people of African descent. I marched on the mall in Washington, DC for equal justice for all African American people.

I grew up in a Christian home where love and respect were practiced, and Christian principals were taught. Church and Sunday school were a "must" and has been a part of my life from the very beginning of my existence. As a child, I was taken to Sunday school and church. As I grew, I became involved in the business of the church, and I have continued throughout my entire life.

My family has been the "bedrock" for my journey. I helped organize our annual family reunions. Having grown up on a farm, I learned many things experientially. I could not fully appreciate them then, but as I reflect on those years, I would not change anything.

Wooten Family

Growing Up Black in Rural North Carolina

My Childhood Home

I was born November 2, 1930, in a community known as Black Swamp in rural North Carolina. I was delivered by a midwife whose name was Agnes Scott. The United States and much of the rest of the world was experiencing the worst economic downturn in the history of the Western Industrialized world. Racial segregation was the law in the South, and the environment was charged with hate and fear. The period between 1929 and 1939 became known as the Great Depression. Farm prices fell so drastically that many farmers lost their houses and land. Some farmers migrated to the cities to look for work. Many food products were rationed, and children were only allowed two pairs of shoes per year. The government found it necessary to issue ration cards so people would not hoard. Canning became a significant focus.

Thank God for my wonderful parents. While they were wholly disrespected by most white people, they maintained their dignity. They had strong faith in God and were very resourceful farmers. They taught us to respect ourselves and others. While they had little academic training, they had plenty of common sense (mother wit).

Papa built our family house. It was a large two-story house that stood way down a long lane. It had five rooms downstairs—kitchen, dining room, mama & papa's bedroom, a family room and a living room separated by the stairs and a hallway. There were two bedrooms upstairs and a wide hallway (used as a bedroom). The house had a long "L" shaped porch on the back, and the front porch stretched nearly all the way across the house. There were swings on both porches. The swings were a lot of fun. The swing in the yard was mounted between two giant tall poles. The chains were sturdy and strong with a rubber inner tube seat. We would sit and swing, and stand up and swing. We could swing really high because the chains were nice and long. This was one of the most enjoyable play activities of my childhood. All the children of the neighborhood loved to play on that swing. Before electric current, there was a fireplace in the living room and a wood-burning heater in the family room, the dining room and bedrooms upstairs. Also, we used wood in the kitchen stove. Wood for the kitchen stove had to be cut into sticks about 10-12 inches long and no more than about two-three inches thick. Wood for the heaters could be much larger, and wood for the fireplace could be longer. We used kerosene lamps and lanterns for light, and potties at night. During the day we used "outhouses."

I never knew my father's parents. However, I know that his mother's name was Harriet, and his father's name was Needham, and my father had three brothers—Council, William, and Needham. My father, Lewis, was the youngest. I was told that my grandmother was pregnant with my father when my grandfather died, so my father never knew his "dad." It must have been challenging for my grandmother raising their four sons as a single parent in that time of segregation.

We are a blended family. My father was married twice. His first wife was named Laura Jane (Mama Laura). They had four children-- Earl, George, Levy, and Lela. Levy was killed in a hunting accident as a teenager, and Lela died before her second birthday. Mama Laura died when their children were quite young.

Papa married my mother, St. Annie (Mama Annie) shortly after Mama Laura's death. I knew both of my mother's parents. My grandfather's name was St. Mark, and my grandmother's name was Charity. They called each other "daisy." Both grandpa and grandma were strong church workers. My grandfather was a senior deacon, and my grandmother was the "mother" of the church. These were both very significant leadership positions in the church, with considerable responsibility.

My grandparents were farmers. They had 13 children. St. Annie (my mother, was the oldest), Lucinda, Ellie, Pearl, Nola, Nettie, Dorothy Bell, Maceo, Hyram, Ray, Clyde, and David. Both Lucinda and Clyde died as infants.

I have no information about my mother's schooling. I know that she was very gifted in so many areas—cooking, sewing, gardening, canning, nursing, etc.

Papa and Mama Annie had nine children—Frank, Needham, Gertrude, Etta, Thelma, Levernia, Bernice, Yvonne, and Marie. Gertrude died an infant. Mama and Papa raised all of us together as one big happy family. There was no distinction. In reality, we did not really grow up together because of the age difference.

Brother Earl (Big Buddy) as we called him, joined the US Army when he became of age and took advantage of the GI Bill to get a college education. I did not know him until I was a teen, because he rarely came home. He was very private—far from frivolous. He was a very kind, peaceful, friendly person, always willing to lend a helping hand. Big Buddy was married twice. I did not know his first wife Elizabeth Green, but I did know Marion Brinsfield. Marion ran a successful daycare center in Winston-Salem, NC. There were no children born to either of these marriages.

Brother George joined the US Army, also. He was our "old standby." He had a good combination of many attributes. He was gentle, never in a hurry, pleasant smile and disposition. He was a good provider. He married Francis Florence Ward, and they had nine children.

I was not yet five and a half years old when **sister Etta** married Clennie Murphy. They went to live with his parent's in Pollocksville, NC. When their son Clennie, Jr. was born, I went to stay with them so that I could watch "the baby" while my sister helped out in the field. After a short stay with his parents, Clennie and Etta moved into their own home "down the field" from his parents. They lived near the river and a railroad track. Clennie used to light the lantern over the trestle bridge each night so the conductor of the train could see how to cross. He always brought me a little bag of coconut candy when he went to the store (white and pink squares). I have lots of memories from my time living with them. After a period of time, they moved to Washington, DC to find better jobs.

Brother Frank joined the US Navy when he reached the proper age. When he was discharged from the Navy, he met and married Martha Mills from Comfort, NC. They had one daughter. We called brother Frank our source of wisdom. He appeared to have a head for business. He could have been just bluffing, but he sure had us fooled.

Sister Thelma went away to a trade school in Elizabeth City, NC, where she learned how to make men's clothes. She married Richard Davis from Warrenton, NC. They were married at our house in Maysville, NC. They went to live with Richard's parents in Warrenton, NC until they were able to buy their own home. I

remember they had to carry water from a spring way, way down the hill from their house because drilling was far too expensive for them to get a pump for a very long time. Their home was on a hill. They had four children. Thelma always reminded us of "family unity." She did not want to be left out.

Sister Levernia went to beauty school and ran a successful beauty shop in Maysville, (next door to my brother George) for a period of time. She married Isaac Franks from the White Oak River community. They had ten children. They lived in the White Oak community in the house where Isaac grew up and worked on their farm. Later they moved to Washington, DC for a time until they decided to return to NC where they built a new house.

Sister Bernice was the first daughter to complete college. She majored in Home Economics at NC A & T College in Greensboro, NC. **Bernice** was named Agriculture Queen by popular vote of her peers. She married Fletcher Barber from Trenton, NC. They have four sons. Bernice worked as the Home Health Agent in

Jones County, and as a teacher in Jones High School until retirement. We called her "the worry wart," because she made her conversation sound like she was worrying. She probably worried far less than any of us.

Brother Needham joined the US Army. Needham married Janie Kinsey from Trenton, NC. They have five children. Needham and Janie had a house built on the family property where only the outside was finished. Needham completed the building and was very skilled in so many areas. He was a fun guy. He was noted for his "dry" humor.

Marie, my youngest sister (the baby), went to college at Winston-Salem, NC. She married Lonell Mattocks of Belgrade, NC. Marie taught

school in the Jones County public schools until her retirement. They have four children. Marie knows how to do lots more things than she gives herself credit for. She is another fun person and has a "new" name for almost everyone. She is quite a girl!

Delilah Yvonne that is me. I remember growing up tall and thin and never having clothes to fit. Much of my wardrobe was hand-me-downs. A woman who lived in New Bern, we called Cousin Honey, worked for white people who would always have a bag of clothes for mama whenever she went to town. I guess we were poor, but I wasn't aware of it. I think that because my clothes did not fit, and perhaps I was ashamed of the way I looked, I was called shy. If my mother had just had enough time to alter my clothes, maybe I would have felt better about myself.

Little girls with long hair were said to be pretty, but I did not think that I was. I really did not like myself. I wore my hair in braids all the way through high school when other girls my age were wearing curls. I got to wear curls on special occasions. I graduated from both elementary and high school as valedictorian. I was the second daughter to complete college at NC A & T College. I majored in Commercial Education. I was voted "Miss A & T"—the college queen, by my peers. I was also May queen that same year.

When I graduated, I was recruited to teach in the public schools of Columbus County, NC, Arnour High School. I worked really hard multi-tasking as a teacher, school secretary, duplicating test and other material for other teachers, and developing a school newsletter. I was rewarded with a certificate as "Teacher of the Year."

After working at Armour High School for two years, I married James Marrow from Rocky Mount, NC. We met as students at A & T College. He was an ROTC cadet at A & T and went directly to active duty after graduation. We got married at my home in Maysville, NC in 1954. I visited him at the military base in Ft. Campbell, KY, that summer. I taught one more year then resigned to travel with him. We have three daughters—Yvette, Karen, and Greta all "Army Brats."

I was a "stay-at-home mom" for a decade while we traveled from Ft. Campbell, KY to Augsburg, Germany, to Washington, DC., Columbus, GA, to Baltimore, MD, and back to Washington, DC. When Jay or Jim (as we called him) was discharged from the Army, we stayed in and around the Washington, DC, Maryland area. He completed a Master's degree and taught school in DC, and was a school counselor in Virginia. I went to work in the Washington District government when our youngest daughter was five years old. After three years, I got a job with the Federal government and worked until my retirement in 1986.

We are a family with many different personalities, this makes a beautiful family. I salute this GREAT BUNCH!

The Marrows

James (Jay), Karen, Yvette, Greta and Yvonne

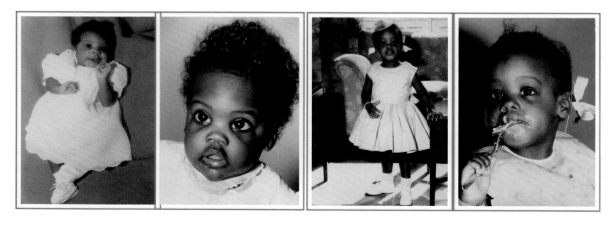

APPRECIATING MY PARENTS

PAPA

My father was a proud man. We called him Papa. Papa was s straight talk "no-nonsense" person. While papa was not privileged to advance beyond the third reader in school, he was very resourceful and a tremendous manager. He was gifted in so many ways. Papa was a very perceptive farmer. It takes skill to know when to plant and rotate your crops to reap the greatest harvest. Papa was a carpenter. Not only did he build our house, but he also built houses and wagons and many different structures for other people. He knew how to drill for water, make molasses, do mule shoeing, basket weaving, and more. Papa was organized and believed in having a place for everything and keeping everything in its place. He was a great economizer. He made everything convenient, so there was no excuse for wasting time shifting from one duty to another. In addition to the pump on the back porch near the kitchen, there was a pump in the barnyard and a pump near the pig pen. There was a well near the laundry house.

Papa built a little house for everything—a small house to do laundry, a little house for the meat (meat was preserved in pork barrels, and papa would hang the smoked meat from the rafters). There was also a place for his carpentry tools. If something was borrowed, it should be returned as soon as its use was finished. The smokehouse and the tool house were built together like a townhouse. Papa built a little house up on stilts called a dairy. That small house was insulated to keep milk, butter, eggs and other perishables fresh. Papa would put a huge block of ice in the little house which lasted at least a week. Of course, there were chicken houses for chickens and stalls/stables for the mules and cows and barns to store the hay and grain. There was a place for farm tools. The same rule applied. He believed in everything being convenient.

Papa was a hunter. Deer was his favorite, but he hunted squirrels, rabbits, birds. The whole family loved fishing. We would dig earthworms and go fishing in the creek way behind our house through the woods. We would catch catfish or eels even perch, robins or pikes. It was a treat to get away from work for a little while. When the shad and herring would swim upstream into the fresh water to spawn, papa would catch lots of them in nets. I remember there were so many herrings, they were dried on the clothesline. This was a way to preserve them. The shad roe was always a delicacy. Mama would scramble it with eggs and serve it with rice. We ate rice with nearly every meal. That shad roe was so good.

Papa made molasses from the juice of sugar cane. We would strip the fodder from the cane, and tie it in bundles for the animals to eat. Then, Papa had a mill that he used to squeeze the juice from the cane. The mill was a series of cogs, where someone had to feed in the stalks a few at a time. A single mule went round and round to make the cogs turn. As the juice was extracted, it was strained into a barrel or several buckets or tubs. Papa made a long contraption (something like a long set of trays hooked together with a little trap door at one end of each tray) to cook the juice into molasses. The cooking contraption was set over a deep pit where a suitable fire was made and kept at just the right temperature for as long as it took to cook a batch of juice into molasses. Skimming off the foam and stoking the fire was a constant three to four-hour vigil until the molasses was just right, and only Papa knew that. The molasses was poured into one-half gallon jars or buckets for sale, and a huge barrel to keep in the barn for family use. Many people from other farms brought cane for Papa to process.

Papa was very creative. Because the mosquitoes and other biting flies were so bad in the summer, he built a "man-sized" crib to sleep in outside. He covered the crib with a screen to allow the air to flow through, but the insects could not get in. (That was a little selfish.) The rest of us had to endure.

Papa was conscientious about our material needs, such as plenty of food year round, and comfortable home, but I do not remember any play. In fact, Papa would stop us from playing if he thought maybe we had not finished our chores. He would find another task and break up our game. Papa believed that "an idle mind was the devil's workshop, so he saw to it that the devil had no workshop with our minds.

Papa died at age 71. I had been home from college doing practice teaching and was scheduled to return to college that weekend when he passed away.

MAMA

Mama was mild-mannered and soft-spoken, but we knew to move when she spoke. I have no information on her schooling, but she was very resourceful. Mama was like a candle. She gave light for all to see. Mama was able to "keep her cool" while juggling all of the many roles and personalities she had to manage. There were at least six of us at home at any given time, plus my father. She had to be a wife, chef, nurse, teacher, seamstress, nurturer, washerwoman, in addition to gardener and farm hand. Mama was a good neighbor. She would lend a hand whenever and wherever she was needed. It is through her wisdom and love that we have such family unity. Everyone loved Mama Annie.

Mama loved her flowers. It didn't matter how much work she had to do in the field, she made time to plant flowers around the house to make the yard beautiful. We had blue and pink hydrangeas, beautiful pink crepe myrtle bushes, orange day-lilies, yellow and white jonquils, cape jasmine bushes and zinnias and verbena and roses and moss and many other shrubs and flowers that I do not remember the names. There was a pecan tree in the corner of the garden next to the house where a wisteria vine twisted itself around, and it bore beautiful purple/blue flowers that hung like bunches of grapes. Those flowers were so beautiful.

Gardening was mostly mama's job. After the men prepared the soil, she would do the planting and weeding and harvesting when the vegetables were ready. Mama was very creative. She canned some of everything including fruits and vegetables, even meat. Mama made preserves from grape hulls, watermelon rinds, and pickles from cucumbers. She made chow chow —a relish. She made jelly and jam. Mama would make the best turnovers and dumplings from the wild berries we picked from around the fence and the edge of the woods. She would serve them hot with homemade ice cream or sweet milk and nutmeg.

Mama made butter from the cream that would rise to the top of the milk. She would put the cream in a churn—this was a big earthenware or thick glass jug that had a plunger with rotary blades made of wood. After churning the cream for a period of time, butter would form and separate from the milk. The milk would have flakes of butter in it. This was called buttermilk. Also, when the skimmed milk set for a couple of days, it would sour and congeal. That was called clabber. Papa loved clabber. He liked to pour molasses over it in his cup and eat it with biscuits. I never did like it. I really did not like milk. On Saturdays Mama and I would take butter and fresh milk (called sweet milk), skimmed milk, buttermilk, clabber, eggs, and fresh vegetables to sell in our little town called Maysville.

Mama died at age 88, during the same month of the family reunion. It was a difficult reunion for all of us.

APPRECIATING MY YEARS GROWING UP ON A FARM

Farming is a seasonal process, and when I was growing up, farming was done with simple mule-drawn tools such as plows, rakes, disk harrows, fertilizer distributors, planters, and muscle-driven tools such as hoes, axes, bush axes, pitchforks, pea diggers, and rakes of many sizes. We had wagons and tobacco trucks and wheelbarrows and buckets, and baskets, everything needed to get the work done. Later, as time moved on, we got a tractor, but still kept a mule for a while.

There was work time and meal time. I really liked that we always ate meals together. We had a huge table that papa built. He built a long bench for one side of the table where the younger children sat by age. Papa sat at the head of the table, and Mama sat next to him on the other side. Those of us on the bench would graduate to a chair when the older sibling left home to work, go away to school, or get married. Manners were taught strictly. If one should finish eating before everyone else, it was proper to ask to be excused from the table. We each took turns asking the blessing before we began eating. We took turns washing and drying dishes. Usually, we took turns in pairs. One would wash and the other dry.

Another of the great things about living in the country on a farm is that most things are learned experientially. We had all kinds of fowl—turkeys, geese, ducks, of all kind of eggs including chickens, turkeys, ducks, chickens, and guineas. I learned about the reproductive process by watching calves, pigs, puppies, and kittens being born. I have watched eggs hatching including wild birds, even snake eggs. I learned all about trees by walking in the woods with my brothers and father. I know about making flour from wheat and meal from ears of corn. We had large barrels of flour and meal in the kitchen that lasted all year long,

We had no lawnmowers. The area of the yard near the house did not have grass. We cut tree branches to sweep that portion of the yard, and the other part was cut with the hay cutter or a sling blade. We had dogs and cats aplenty, and the foul ran loose in the yard, so there were lots of flies. It was hard to finish a meal without having a fly dip into the gravy or whatever dish was on the table. Mama would politely remove the bowl to the kitchen, dip the fly out and return the dish to the table. I do not think anyone thought anything about it. We just kept right on with our meal.

Some of the daily chores included milking the cows, and driving them to the pastures for the day, feeding and providing water for the fowl and livestock, making sure there was enough wood stacked on the porch for the heaters and the kitchen stove. We needed to make sure all of the lamps were filled with kerosene, and the lamp shades were washed. Of course, plowing and cultivating the crops in the garden and field.

There were many trees around our farm. There was a chinaberry tree in the front yard where we would sit in its shade, and whenever we had company. We had fruit trees all over the property—several varieties of apple trees, pear trees, plumb, peach, and fig. There were pecan trees in the yard and walnut and hickory nut trees in the edge of the woods. There were a mulberry tree and a persimmon tree way down in the field. Papa would make persimmon beer when the persimmons were ripe, but as children were not allowed to drink it. It was just for grownups, and probably only the men. There were wild huckleberries and blueberries and blackberries on the fence. We would have a great time eating grapes from the harbor in the garden when the season was just right.

There were a lot of fun things to do as well. I was often called a Tom Boy because I preferred outdoor activities and chores rather than being inside the house. I am a risk taker. I climbed trees and fences. You might find me perched on a limb in our chinaberry tree that spread its lofty limbs to provide shade in our front yard. Needham made pop pistols from the shank of the bamboo that grew near our backyard. We were not able to hit anything, but hearing the loud pop was fun. I could play marbles, hitch mules, and was the guinea pig for many of my brother's creations. He and I were best buddies. We played together and did chores together.

When there would come a torrential downpour of rain, and the ditches through the field and the yard would overflow their banks, the yard would be flooded, and you could catch me running barefoot through muddy water. We always went barefoot from May until the chilly

weather in September, except on Sunday. The main reason was that it saved money on buying shoes, and the other reason was it was just not easy to keep them from getting full of dirt. No need to have feet and dirt in the same shoes. Sometimes the sole of the shoe would come off and would be flapping when we walked. So, why not just take off the shoes.

We would catch minnows and tadpoles from the ditch in a jar. We would also catch fireflies in a jar and watch their magic. He would build carts or other contraptions. Many times he would hitch the dog to the cart. He would make traps to catch birds. He built a "playhouse" for me. We used our imagination. I used bottle caps and broken dishes, and bottles and cans to stock my kitchen. If there was an old cushion, I used it as a sofa. Our food consisted of pork berry and dandelion leaves. Wood chips were the meat. We would talk with imaginary people. We would have school or church in that little playhouse now and then.

Childhood diseases did not escape me. I had measles and mumps and chicken pox, and on top of all of that, I ran into a hornet's nest and got stung all over. My brother and I were chasing the cows to the woods where they stayed and grazed all day. So much pain for such a little girl, but you couldn't stop me from following my brother around.

HOG KILLING

Slaughtering hogs and cattle was done in the winter months because it was cold enough to preserve the meat since there was no refrigerators or freezers. This was always a big neighborhood production. Almost always four or five hogs would be slaughtered in one day.

Papa would instruct my brothers on how to dig a huge hole large enough to hold a big hog, they would anchor a vat in the hole, and fill it with water to scald the hog. Wood and kindling were placed under the vat to heat the water. On the actual day of the "hog killing," Papa would get my brothers up really early to light the fire so the water would get very, very hot before the hogs were killed.

After the hogs were scalded, the hair would be scraped off, and they would hang them on a gallows to wash them and finish cleaning them. They would remove the intestines and other internal organs(liver, heart, kidneys, etc.) The men did the butchering—trimming the hams, shoulders, the loin, and ribs, and separating the shanks. The head and feet were set aside for further cleaning. They would cut away the fat in slabs. The women cut the fat in smaller pieces to rend for lard. The women, also, cleaned the chitterlings and made the sausage. We used the big black wash pot to rend the fat. I liked sampling the sausage as it was being seasoned and tested.

We would begin early in the morning and work until after dark. Not too much was done after dark because lamp light was too weak to assure safety and sanitation

SUNDAYS

On Sunday, we dressed up and went to Sunday School and church after having prayer at home around the breakfast table. Usually, one of my older siblings would read a passage of Scripture from the Bible. Each of us would say a Bible verse followed by Mama saying a prayer and blessing the food. Everyone was expected to assemble around the table together, and eat whatever was prepared for that particular meal. We would clean up the kitchen after breakfast, then head off to the church house. We walked because it was not very far, and besides, we did not have a car for a very long time. There was no question about Sunday School or church, it was a given.

The preacher came only one Sunday each month, but we had Sunday school every Sunday. I never questioned the older people, the preacher or the Bible. I had faith that whatever was said or whatever I read was the truth, and I was not to question it. When I look back now, from my current vantage point, I wonder how my life would have been different had I questioned some of the religious values that were taught in Sunday School, church, at home, and at school.

Believing in the Golden Rule has stood me in good stead over the years, i.e. "Do unto others as you would have them do unto you."

Bernice, Mama, Papa, Yvonne, Needham and Marie

Grandma Charity and Mama Annie

Tobacco
North Carolina's Cash Crop

Tobacco was our chief money crop, and it took a lot of preparation. Preparation began with the cutting of the ground with a disk harrow, then plowing the spot where the tobacco seeds would be planted. The mule-drawn rake would be used to remove any large roots or rocks, then we would rake the area with the pea digger or other small rakes until the soil was completely free of all sticks, large lumps or dirt, rocks or roots. When the ground was considered ready, Papa would mix the tobacco seeds along with a little fertilizer and sand then spread this mixture evenly over the prepared soil.

A leaf rake was used to mix the seeds and fertilizer with the soil gently. A frame was built around the entire area then a layer of cheesecloth was stretched and nailed over the seeding area. Extra care was taken to keep out birds and animals or anything that would disturb the seeds. After several weeks the seeds would sprout and come up along with the weeds and grass. Then there was the tedious job of carefully picking out the weeds and grass by hand. This would take days. We would place a longboard across the frame around the seeded area to keep from stepping on any seedlings. It was a back-breaking job, and you dare not step in the bed or pull any tobacco plants by mistake. After the first picking of weeds, the cover was returned until another growth of the plants and weeds. When the plants were approximately four inches tall, the cloth would be removed altogether so the plants could gain strength from the sun. If the soil were too dry, we would haul water to the area and gently spray the plants, never at hard force. When the plants were finally large enough and strong enough, they were transplanted in the field where rows had been prepared.

First, the ground was cut up with the disk harrow. Usually, my brother would cut the field several times alternating crosswise and straight up and down so that the soil was thoroughly pulverized. Then the plow was used to make deep straight furrows evenly spaced—approximately 4 to 6 feet apart. Then fertilizer was put in the grooves with a particular fertilizer distributor. Seems like hundreds of bags of fertilizer were hauled in by Mr. Aman—the man Papa had an account with for all his farm supplies. After the fertilizer was put in, then the plow was used to cover the fertilizer. First, a furrow was turned from the left side then another from the right side making a sharply pointed ridge. When everything was ready, a board was fastened to the rake and to flatten the surface. Here is when another back-breaking job would begin.

Someone would drop plants about 15-18 inches apart, and another person would come along with a peg to actually put the plants in the ground by making a hole, cutting the plant in and covering the hole. Another person would put water around the plant. The peg was approximately 12 inches long and tapered like a sharpened pencil. Bending down like this all day long was no fun. You would feel like your back was breaking.

This was just the beginning. After the plants had time to catch roots, we'd go through the field to notice where some had died. This was another job for the girls. We'd carry a bucket with plants and another bucket with water. The dead plant was removed and a new plant put in that space.

As technology advanced, my father kept pace. The next planting tool I remember was a mechanical hand-held planting machine that could hold water. It was made of tin and had a pointed bottom with a spring snap opening to allow the plant and water to be released in the hole at the same time. It took two people to operate the planting successfully. The person working the planter would jab the planter in the ground, the other person would drop the plants in the proper opening. This was much faster and not as much work and was a "stand up" operation. This really saved our backs. Of course, as time moved on, tractors replaced mules, and the use of pesticides cut down on weeds and grass.

There are many, many more phases to the tobacco story before it was ready for sale at the auction. There was breaking the flowering tops, picking the worms and chopping the grass and weeds. Then there was harvesting, and curing and grading, and tying the dried tobacco into small bunches called "hanks." When all of these steps were finished, the hanks were fastened in burlap sheets by shades—usually about six different colors—shades of yellow and brown, and shades of green. The prices were different for each shade. The lighter the color, the better the price.

Time passed. Now there are hardly any "small farmers." All you see now are the mega tractors with self-planters, and the entire stalk is cut and cured instead of one leaf at a time as it was done in "my day." Pesticides have replaced the chopping and picking worms, etc. There is no wonder so many people are getting cancer from using tobacco products.

Elementary and High School JONES COUNTY, NC

It was just about a quarter of a mile from our house to the one-room Rosenwald School where I attended my first six grades in school. We would take a shortcut through the woods and pick honeysuckers and huckleberries in season. There were even some little red sweet peppermint berries we would pick. Sometimes we would collect rosin from the gum tree. It was like chewing gum. In the springtime, there was a very sweet smell of jasmine in the air. We would pull the jasmine vines for jump rope, at school, and at home. We had lots of fun playing with all the other neighborhood children on the roadway walking to and from school.

Our teacher was very talented. She taught all six grades in that one room with minimal discipline problems. She coordinated the work so that everyone was busy all day.
We played games at recess—jump rope and ring games were the most popular. We had talent shows on Friday and plays at the end of the school year.

In 1941, that school was consolidated due to a Court Order (Brown vs. the Board of Education), and we had to ride the school bus about three miles one way to school. We had to walk about a quarter mile to wait for the school bus. The bus was often late. The driver had to pick up children who lived much further away than our pick up location. The reason we had to walk so far, and the bus was late so often was due to racial segregation. White children got the new busses and were picked up in front of their home, and their school was a much shorter distance away. Black children got the used busses that were not in good condition and had to ride past the white school to get to our destination. We even got the books that had been used by the white children. Many of the books were written in and pages torn, but we were to protect them as if they were new.

There were lots more students and teachers at the new school, and they were much more sophisticated than I. There was lots of dating, and some of the students were smoking. Often I felt left out. Occasionally, I tried to join in, but it was difficult.
I was a good student. Spelling and arithmetic were my favorite subjects. I remember memorizing lots of poems and Bible verses. Our homeroom teacher was my cousin, and he was a preacher. Devotions and Bible lessons were part of the school schedule when I was in elementary and high school.

I had terrible headaches in the eighth grade. The doctor said it was sinus. Sometimes, I would leave school and go to rest at my brother George's house, until school was over for the day. I graduated from the eighth grade as valedictorian of my class.

High school was 8 – 10 miles away from where I lived. Again, we walked about a quarter mile to get to our pickup point. When the weather was cold, we would go inside the little store where we waited for the bus. The store owner was white, and he was not very happy about having us inside his store. Everything was segregated. Tardiness at school was a common occurrence.

By the time I entered high school, I had learned to cope with being alone, Everything moved very fast. I felt like an "oddball." I wore my dresses longer than the other girls, my hair in braids, and bows on my hair. I had nothing to share about dating. These things kept me isolated. Since I did not have money, I brought my lunch from home. Again, I felt left out. Quiet people often get left out. I graduated from high school as valedictorian.

The Rosenwald Schools: Schools for African-Americans in the Rural South

College Life
A & T State College
Greensboro, NC
1948-1952

College years were especially challenging for me. I had low, low self-esteem, but I was able to mask it successfully. I missed almost all the meals on Sunday at the dining hall, because I did not want to be scrutinized by the guys sitting in front of the cafeteria.

I make friends easily, and I had a lot of friends. I have stayed in touch with a few of my classmates over the years. I was a good student. I worked part-time to help pay for my tuition and books. My sister Bernice helped me too because my parents were not able to pay for all of my expenses.

I will never know how I became so popular as to be chosen the college queen as well as May queen, and the Phi Beta Sigma fraternity queen. I never thought I deserved these honors. All choices were made by popular vote. Everybody kept telling me how my family would support me. Well, that much was true, but they had no money help expand my wardrobe for the extra activities I was expected to attend. Since my wardrobe was minimal, I made a couple of outfits including the dress I wore as May queen. It was a long and white dress made of organza material. The President's reception for seniors was that same evening. So, after reigning as May Queen, I went back to the dorm and cut it short for the reception. That was pretty ingenious. If I must say so myself.

My father had a stroke at the end of my sophomore year. I missed the first quarter of my junior year because I was needed to stay home and help out on the farm. I went to summer school to make up the quarter I missed so I could graduate along with my senior class.

I moved off campus my senior year. I lived in the home of the Stanley's. I worked for Rev. Stanley after school. He was the Superintendent of the Southern District Conference of the Christian Churches. I was glad to be staying off campus because I would not be seen as much. You see, as the college queen "Miss A & T," I should attend many functions. I was nervous each time something came up where I had to be present or speak. There were several functions where I definitely had to attend—The Capital Classics (football game) played in Washington, DC was one of them. I had to parade on the football field at half-time. When it came time for homecoming, I had to borrow things to wear, and Mrs. Stanley helped me make my suit for the football game. Fortunately, I was able to open an account at one of the department stores so I could buy accessories and something to wear after the game.

It was customary for the reigning "Miss A & T" and the president of the student council to lead the graduating seniors at commencement. Again, I needed a white suit. I actually borrowed the white outfit I wore from the former Miss A & T. I used my ingenuity to get through a very tough year.

Miss A & T

SPEECH GIVEN AT THE A & T HOMECOMING GAME 1951

President Bluford, Fellow Students, Alumni, and Friends:

In the life of every person who is interested in education, whether he/she be student, alumnus, or friend, homecoming is a grand occasion for all who attend. So, once again we are glad to participate in the Homecoming at The Agricultural and Technical College in Greensboro, North Carolina. As your Miss A & T, it is a real pleasure for me to greet you.

To the faculty members, students and football team of Florida A & M College, we extend to you, on behalf of the administrative staff, the entire student body and alumni, of A & T College, a most cordial welcome. And in all sincerity, we want to make the whole student body, the alumni, and all friends of the college welcome. I hope that you will feel, with me, the joy and happiness that this occasion always brings.

To our famous football team, we wish the greatest success for each man. May this Homecoming be remembered as one of the most outstanding in the history of our college. Win or lose, may the spirit of good sportsmanship, which is characteristic of A & T College, permeate every heart.

None of you could be more elated than I, on this thrilling occasion and we want everyone to feel perfectly at home—meet your friends and make this day to be long remembered. May the spirit of loyalty and unity dwell in your hearts as you go forward, and may this day be an inspiration to you.

Miss
Iota
Phi
Lambda

The Delta Theta Chapter of the Iota Phi Lambda Sorority of A. and T. College observed its annual Thanksgiving project by carrying clothing to the Juvenile Department. Shown here from left to right, are: Misses Gloria Jennings, Yvonne Wooten and Dollie Chapman.

Student of the Month

Yvonne Wooten, born November 2, 1930, the daughter of Mr. and Mrs. Lewis Wooten of Maysville, North Carolina. Miss Wooten graduated from high school at Pollocksville in the spring of 1948. While there she participated in the choral group, won a metal for the best typist, and was valedictorian for her class.

She entered this institution in the fall of 1948, majoring in Commercial Education, which has been her interest since she entered high school.

Her freshman year, she was the "Crescent's Club Sweetheart." She is secretary of the Iota Phi Lambda Sorority, a member of the Sunday School, Y. W. C. A., The Business Association, and secretary of the Junior-Senior Council.

This year she was "Miss Junior Class," "Miss Second Battalion," "Miss May Queen," and Second Maid of Honor to "Miss Co-ed," and is "Miss A. and T. for 1951-52."

Among her hobbies: Movies, sewing, music, entertaining and all types of sports. Also she likes to type. She has been employed on the campus as part-time worker in the library, secretary to Dr. George, and secretary to Dr. A. P. Graves, head of the Biology Department. Her life's ambition is to become an ~~efficient secretary~~.

She is always willing to share with others her knowledge. Her knowledge is very extended.

HOWARD L. WARD

——— 0 ———

Picture
above

May
Queen

Congratulations

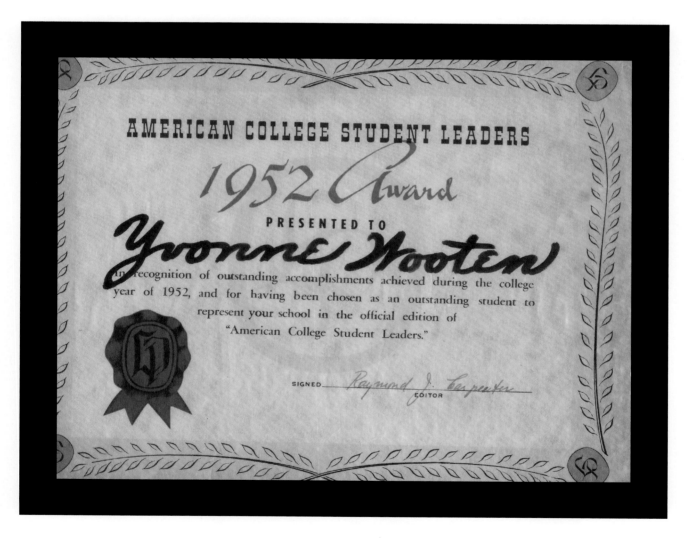

AMERICAN COLLEGE STUDENT LEADERS

1952 Award

PRESENTED TO

Yvonne Wooten

In recognition of outstanding accomplishments achieved during the college year of 1952, and for having been chosen as an outstanding student to represent your school in the official edition of "American College Student Leaders."

SIGNED *Raymond J. Carpenter*
EDITOR

This is to Certify that

Yvonne Wooten

has been selected to appear in the
1951=52 Edition of

Who's Who Among
Students

In American Universities and Colleges

from

Agricultural and Technical College
of North Carolina

This honor comes in recognition of the merit and accomplishment of the student who was officially recommended by the above named institution and met the requirements of this publication.

H. Pettus Randall
EDITOR

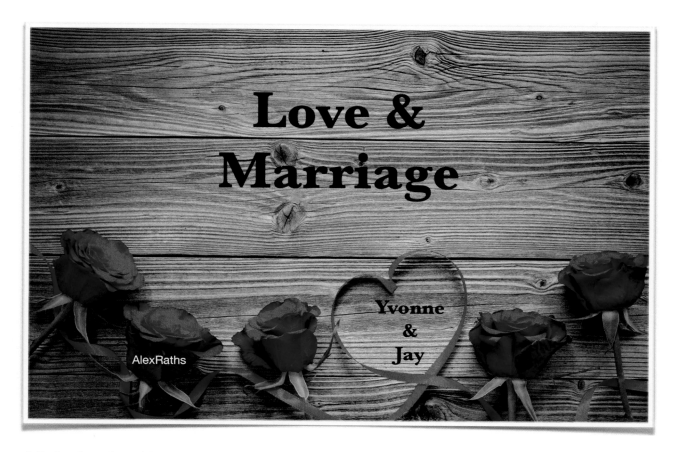

Love &
Marriage

Yvonne
&
Jay

AlexRaths

My husband and I met at NC A&T College where we were both students. We were casual friends. We took a couple of classes together, went to the movies a few times, but nothing serious during our years at college. Each of us was dating someone else and had preliminary plans to marry the person we were dating until something changed. I lost interest in the man I was dating, and he too made a change in his commitment to the person he was dating.

It was the end of the school year. I graduated and was recruited to teach at Armour High School in Armour, NC. He had another year before graduating from college. We each went our separate ways. The following summer after he graduated and was commissioned to the Army, he wrote a letter to me at my home address from his military post. The letter was forwarded to me in Atlantic City, NJ, where I was visiting my uncle for a few weeks.

I leaped with excitement when I received the letter because I had no idea he would ever communicate with me again after school. As I recall, there was no return address, but I got his home address from our yearbook. So sometime near the end of the summer I wrote and sent my letter to his mother so she could forward it to him. This was the beginning of a regular correspondence between us which resulted in a proposal to marry. At that time all of our dates had been through the mail. He came to my home to visit for my birthday. His uncle "CM" brought him. They lived about 100 miles away in Rocky Mount, NC. We stayed up late talking about school and looking at old yearbooks. As far as I was concerned, we were not really behaving like a couple thinking of marriage. As a matter of fact, I don't think we even kissed that night. This was great for me because I never liked a lot of "touching."

He went back to his military base, and I back to my school. We continued to write about once or twice a month. He came home again for Easter. He wanted me to visit his home, and meet his folk, so we planned it, and I went. I think I went up on the bus. It was the Easter weekend.

This time, he made a real proposal. We talked about everything, and when he finally (popped the question) asked me to marry him, I hesitated for a long while before I said yes. He told me later how nervous that made him when I didn't respond right away.

From that moment on, I recall adopting the stereotyped role of the excited bride-to-be. I was floating on "cloud 9" all day. He bought a lovely corsage for me to wear to church. I am sure I beamed beautifully as any bride-to-be would. Later that day when he took me home, I told my mother. Being the concerned mother, she inquired right away if I were sure this is what I wanted to do. I assured her it was, and so the date was set, and plans for the wedding commenced.

I remember being so excited about the wedding, I often forgot to introduce him to family or friends we would meet. We knew very little about each other, but I was sure it would be fun to explore this new personality. After all, I knew just exactly what I wanted.

I remember my fantasy as a child was to get married, have three children spaced about two years apart. I looked forward to being a "housewife" in my imagination. I had thought about what it would be like to prepare meals for my husband, and take care of my children while keeping a comfortable and convenient lovely clean home. Well, things did not work out the way I had fantasized at all. First of all, I was disappointed with my marriage right from the start. My husband was not as affectionate or passionate or as open with his feelings as I. Instead of us talking about how we felt, each of us kept our feelings to ourselves. Although, I did try to share some of what I felt, mostly I internalized the pain, and assumed that whatever was wrong was all my fault. We stayed with his uncle and aunt in Rocky Mount on our wedding night. We had married in Maysville at my parent's home where I grew up, and his best man drove us to Rocky Mount where this uncle and aunt lived.

He was in the Army stationed at Ft. Campbell, KY. I was teaching school in Columbus County, Armour, NC, and was on summer break. We had gotten married on June 21, 1954. We had planned to drive to KY where I would stay until school started in August. He had a little Studebaker. I had prepared for the trip. I had made a few outfits. I was so very conservative (you might say "old fashioned"). I bought a little white pique hat to wear with my red and blue jumper dress made for the trip.

We packed up this little Studebaker, and he drove from Rocky Mount for as long as he could until he was so sleepy and tired we had to stop along beside the road for a quick nap. Then he drove again until he could no longer make it. He was exhausted. I remember we had reached the mountains of Tennessee. I had never driven in the mountains, and I was petrified. When we finally got through the mountains the brakes were burned out. Fortunately, we did not have an accident, and we were able to get the brakes fixed. It was a long drive, and we were both worn out by the time we reached the base.

It turned out to be a very long and disappointing summer. He was in the field overnight a lot, and I was not satisfied with our relationship at all. We shared an apartment with another couple of newlyweds who were very nice. The husband was one of my husband's classmates from A & T. We got along beautifully. I was on vacation from school, so I stayed home and rested while my husband worked. When he came home pooped out, I was pepped up and ready to go. It was this miss match that caused a lot of frustration for both of us. We passed little put down remarks back and forth instead of looking at the reality and talking about it. We would patch up our differences somehow and keep going. Because of the traditional societal roles for women and men we had adopted, I think we each had certain expectations. When those expectations were not met, disappointment set in and feelings came up that were never resolved. We kept creating new situations and putting the feelings away. I am aware that I blamed myself for a lot of what was taking place. I was glad when the summer was over in one way, and on the other hand, I was frustrated that things did not go well and what could I have done differently to make it better.

We played cards a lot and entertained friends a lot. I remember wanting to walk around at night or go dancing and not getting the opportunity because this was not the favorite thing for everyone else. When the summer was over, it was back to school.

That year was difficult for me. I was not happy at the school, and besides, I wanted to get on with making our family. I had lots of time to think and plan what we would do when we were together. I had pretty definite ideas about my goals for the marriage, so I set out to fulfill them. When we were together at Christmas vacation, I shared my thoughts. As I reflect on what happened throughout our marriage, it is clear that I always shared my feelings with him. He was never quite so generous. I always felt I was prying into his private life to raise questions about what he was feeling. I wanted him to share his background, but he always wanted to change the subject and usually did. Later I discovered why. His family of origin was very different than mine, and I suspect he did not know how I would respond to his reality. I think my openness probably made him more insecure, so he became defensive at times. I really did not understand at the time, and I did not know how to handle this. I knew I was uncomfortable and wanted very much for things to be different. I poured on more affection which appeared to be the wrong thing. I began to feel that I would not be able to do anything right. You see, I had adopted the powerless role of thinking I was supposed to "make my man happy." I really tried to reach out. These were difficult times for our marriage.

School was over for the year, and I packed my bags and went to Kentucky. I looked forward to this summer because it was time for us to begin our family. The summer was very frustrating. We talked about starting our family, but when we tried nothing happened. I had expected that I would get pregnant the first time we did not use contraceptives. Well, it did not happen, so I began to worry that something was wrong with me. I worried a lot. Also, I had an ulterior motive, I had planned to use pregnancy as an excuse to resign from my teaching assignment.

Before the summer was over, it finally happened. I was so excited. I was also very sick. I would eat, and everything would come back very shortly. I got pleurisy and was so afraid I was going to miscarry. I was miserable all summer. One night about midnight I felt like eating a hot dog from one of the nearby hot dog stands. I asked my husband to take me out or go get one for me. He thought it was very funny, and refused to do either. I thought that was very inconsiderate of him, and I never really forgave him for that cruelty. He was not very affectionate with me anyway. He teased me about being sick in the presence of our friends.

I resigned from school, and this was the beginning of the family routine. It was stay at home and cook and clean or sleep or crochet. Most of the time I was bored just sitting around by myself.

Just before our first child was due, he received orders to go overseas to Germany. I was too far advanced in my pregnancy to accompany him, so I stayed with my sister in Washington, DC. It was near Valentine's Day when I left Ft. Campbell. He sent me one dozen long stem roses. This was a surprise because he never did little things like that for me. I loved it. (After 24 years, three daughters, a lot of traveling from one military base to another, I decided this was enough. So, I decided we would probably be happier living separately than together. We were divorced in September 1978.)

Me and the Gang!

Parenting
One of my Defining Moments
"Pregnancy and Birth of My 3 Children"

There is a lot of joy and many, many challenges in being a parent. Both partners should prepare for parenting. I think there should be a desire for this role for one to be a good parent. One's mental attitude is critical. Questions about what is right often come up, or what should I do in this situation. Does anyone know what is right? I think what is right is what happens when both parents are happy in their relationship with God and with each other. They are free then to be and let be -- love is natural and is shared fully.

I am a parent. I have enjoyed many happy times, although most of my early years were very frustrating. I remember wanting everything to be just right. I wanted my little girls to be happy, well mannered, pretty and loving. I wanted them to be smart, witty and creative. They were, and still are all of these things. Each has her own personality, and it is beautiful. They sometimes have difficulty letting their real beauty show because of the tremendous hurt they have received. While they are not little girls anymore, sometimes they need parenting advice. Parenting is challenging. Young people have stimulating minds. They are full of ideas and tricks, and always eager to pass them out or try them out on parents. "I believe that children are our future." They will be our world tomorrow.

Yvette, Karen & Greta

Cheremuha

The Butterfly

Beginning in the early nineteen seventies, I felt like I was in a cocoon. Nothing significant was happening in my life. I planned a family vacation. We took a trip out west to California. We had a marvelous time. We visited three major cities along the Pacific coast—San Diego, Los Angeles, and San Francisco. We visited longtime friends living in the Los Angeles area. That little vacation gave me the boost I needed to get moving.

Our family reunion was held in Washington, DC, June 1972. I joined Re-Evaluation Counseling (RC) and Toastmasters—both organizations are designed to help strengthen one's confidence and help maintain a clear focus. Trying to break out of that cocoon was not easy, but I was beginning to grow. I could feel the pulls and stretches of change. I needed to make some difficult decisions if I was ever to break out. I began to let go on old habits and many of the things I was expected to do. It was not easy for the people around me or me.

By 1976, I had fully shed the cocoon and was ready to fly. I decided to make significant changes in my life. To help me move, I took a training course entitled "Mid-Life/Mid-Career Planning." In that same year, I returned to my college homecoming, and a "Roundup of Queens." It had been 24 years since my graduation and my reign as college queen.

I made a major decision to move into an apartment separate from my husband. I bought a new car, and I was feeling like a new person. I started to participate more with the Revaluation Counseling organization, and with the national setting of the United Church of Christ (UCC). I was elected delegate to the General Synod (the bi-annual decision-making body of the denomination). I was elected President of the Black Women's Caucus at that meeting. This was the first national office I had ever held. I went to the World Conference of RC as a delegate— the policy and guidelines body for the international community.

In 1978, I moved to Washington, DC, where everything was very convenient. I walked to work, and I was living very close to public transportation. My calendar and my travel log were very full. This butterfly was beginning to really fly. In January, I took a training lab on becoming a change agent. I left that event before it was over to join the National UCC Women's Conference In Cincinnati, OH (already in progress). I returned home really motivated. I became aware of the lack of Black women in the decision-making process of the church. As President of Black Women's Caucus of the UCC, I was determined to help change that reality. I could hear the "Spirit of God" speaking to me and directing me. I began to work on a. proposal for implementing my vision. I could not do things fast enough. I felt like I was "running from my shadow." Not only was I working full time, but I was also participating more fully in church activities and RC. I went as a delegate to the RC world conference for the second time, and to the General Synod of the UCC for a second term, and I was ordained as a Deacon in my local church.

The project for training Black women was named, "Empowerment for Change." The goals of the project were: to provide opportunities for basic skills in leadership development; to establish communication channels for information sharing; to gather Black women periodically for building mutual sharing and resource development, and to hear, witness and minister in the spirit of Christ. Our personal goals were to become skilled Black women able to, be actively involved on church boards, at the local, association, conference and the national settings; to develop background experiences to serve as a network and as resource leaders in local and kindred churches; and to bear witness and minister in the spirit of Christ. As coordinator of the project, there were so many things to do—apply for funding, recruit participants, and on and on.

The project was designed to cover a two year period, with recruitment targeted at crucial parishes throughout the conference. Our goals were accomplished. Eight women completed the project. Our presence made a significant impact in the church. All of us moved into significant leadership easily in all settings of the church. The project was a huge success.

Our family reunion theme for 1980 was "The Wooten Family Stretching into the 80's." Indeed, I was relieved to close the decade of the 70's. I "flew into the 80's" with confidence, bravery, and a new outlook on life. I haven't stopped soaring. I am so thankful to God for this everlasting love. "It's up, up, and away. Fly butterfly, fly!".

Warawirl

The Flight of the Butterfly
(Butterfly on the Move)

The ever elusive "They" say "A Rolling Stone Gathers no Moss." I guess I have proven "They" to be somewhat correct. I sometimes feel like a "Rolling Stone." While I have not gathered any moss, "so to speak," I have gained so much more. I have lots of friends and so much experience that I would not trade for any amount of moss.

I started rolling when I left home in 1948 to matriculate at North Carolina Agricultural & Technical College (A&T) in Greensboro, North Carolina. I moved off campus my senior year to live with the Stanley family who also lived in Greensboro, North Carolina.

After graduating in 1952, I was recruited to teach at Armour High School in Armour, North Carolina (Columbus County). I lived in the home of a community resident near the school.

The next big move was to live with my military husband who was stationed at Ft. Campbell, Kentucky We got married in 1954. Two years later, he received orders for Augsburg, Germany with Operation Gyroscope. I waited until our first daughter was born, Cheryl Yvette, at Walter Reed Army Medical Center in Washington, DC. Six weeks later we joined my husband in Augsburg. Our second daughter, Karen Denise, was born May 8, 1957, in Augsburg.

When the four of us returned to the United States in 1959, my daughters and I stayed in Washington, DC, while my husband went to Ft. Slocum, New York on a temporary assignment. When his duty was over, we moved to Columbus, Georgia, where he was stationed at Ft. Benning, Georgia.

My husband received orders to teach ROTC at Morgan State College in Baltimore, Maryland in 1960. Our third daughter, Greta Jeanne was born on August 12, 1960, at John Hopkins University Hospital in Baltimore. When Greta was two years old, we moved to Fairmont Street, in Washington, DC. My husband commuted to Ft. Belvoir, Virginia, until his discharge on April 5, 1963. We moved to a larger house on Franklin Street in Washington, DC in 1965.

The next significant move was to Greenwich Woods Apartments in Silver Spring, Maryland. From there, Karen and I moved in 1977, to Springhill Lake Apartments in Greenbelt, Maryland.

My husband and I were divorced in September 1978. I moved to Town Center Apartments in Southwest Washington, DC to live alone. In 1985, the management of Town Center changed from apartments to condominiums. It was time for me to get housing that was a little more stable. So, I moved from that building to buy a condo at Riverside Drive, in Southwest, Washington, DC.

At the end of February 1986, I retired from the Federal Government. I worked part-time jobs for a couple of years. Then, I decided to relocate back to North Carolina, my home state—where I grew up in Maysville (Black Swamp Community).
In 1988, I moved to New Bern, North Carolina, in transition, while I made plans to purchase a mobile home and settle near the old family house in Maysville. My plan for moving near the old house was to restore the house, convert it into a small retreat center and live there forever after. It took about a year before everything was ready for the move

to Maysville, North Carolina My brother, who lived near, helped to prepare the yard for planting grass and flowers, and he made a space for gardening.

My brand new two bedroom mobile home was anchored less than 10 yards from the old house in 1989. I planted grass and flowers in the yard and had a productive vegetable garden on the back side. I canned and gave away lots of produce. I was doing just what I had dreamed of. Friends from out-of-town came to visit as well as "home folk." We played bid whist at every opportunity. Everything was going so well until it was obvious my plan for restoration of the house was not going to materialize. I was so disappointed that I could not fulfill my dream of restoring the old homestead. Therefore, in 1992, I made arrangements for my mobile home to be moved from "down the field" near the old house, to the front of the property near Catfish Lake Road.

My sister Etta and other family members came from Washington, DC, for a special program at church the same weekend that I moved. On the way back to Washington, DC, my sister had a severe stroke and had to be hospitalized in Kinston, North Carolina immediately. After a short stay in Kinston, my nephew (her only son) made arrangements for her to be transferred via ambulance to Washington, DC. He asked me to stay with her until he was able to find appropriate care for her. When he was able to secure caregiving around the clock for my sister, I returned to North Carolina. I would return to Washington often to give the caregiver a break, and to support my nephew. His father had passed a few years earlier. My sister passed away in October 1997, while I was caring for her. I stayed at her house for a few months afterward.

When I returned to North Carolina, things were not the same. There were no job opportunities or regular activities near where I was living. I soon got bored. So once again in 1998, I decided to return to Washington, DC where it felt more like home, and the opportunities for involvement were greater. I had been back only one year when an opportunity for part-time work in Philadelphia, Pennsylvania came knocking. I seized the opportunity and moved to Korman Suites in Philadelphia in a one bedroom apartment. I went to work right away at St. Joseph's Hospital part-time where my daughter Greta had received medical training. The job was perfect for me.

In 2001, I downsized to a studio apartment in the same complex. Unfortunately, in less than one year, my apartment was vandalized, and I did not feel safe living there any longer. I moved to Korman Suites in Blackwood, New Jersey, near my daughter's home. After two years commuting to work from New Jersey to Philadelphia, I thought it was time for me to settle down and stop moving. After all, I was then over 70 years old. I felt a retirement community was the place for me. I researched several locations in and around Maryland. Why Maryland? I wanted to be near one daughter, convenient to public transportation, and I have lots of family and friends living in that area.

When my research was complete in 2003, I chose The Oaks in Silver Spring, Maryland. This would be a place where "like-minded" people would share many things in common, I thought. However, I did not close my options to the possibility of moving again. I also thought I would bring a fresh perspective to retirement living. I was really happy there for a long time. I loved the location of my apartment and my neighbors. This place was convenient to grocery stores, a branch of the Post Office and I was just five minutes away from my new church home. There was an Activities Director who planned a variety of choices for participation with neighbors. The first three years were great. Then something changed. The management was not as efficient as when I first arrived, and there were hardly any planned activities. It was hard to find neighbors who had as much energy and enthusiasm as I had. I was getting restless again. I needed a fresh start—new surroundings, people with more energy. My mind started racing— Where could I go? What am I looking for? Etc.

It was time to discard some of the "stuff" I had accumulated over the past six years. I prayed I used RC, I journaled, finally a decision. Return to North Carolina again. This time choose Jacksonville—the home of the largest Marine base in the United States. There will be plenty of activity in and around that city, and I will be about 15 minutes from my oldest daughter and my only sister. I made an appointment with my nephew, Charles, who had moved me many times over the years. We settled on December 19, 2009. It was exciting to be moving again.

There came a 16-inch snow storm in the area and much more up and down the East Coast. Therefore, we had to wait until it was safe to drive. The moving date was changed to December 28, 2009. We packed the U-Haul on Monday evening December 28, 2009, we had plenty of help. On Tuesday morning December 29, 2009, bright and early, my nephew Charles drove the U-Haul, and his two sons rode with him. Karen and I rode in a rental car. I had to return to Maryland because I had not finished checking out. After the U-Haul was returned in New Bern, North Carolina, everyone rode in the rental car back to Maryland.

That move was to transitional housing for two and one-half months. By the time I found just the right apartment in Jacksonville, it was March 2010. A good thing I leave my options open for moving because I had not finished yet.

In 2013 my children decided, and I agreed, it was time to stop living alone. While I was doing just fine and loving it, we agreed it was better to relocate with one of them. So, I packed up once again to live in New Jersey with Greta. Greta came with a driver for the U-Haul on Friday night, April 20. We packed the U-Haul early Saturday morning, with lots of help, and went on our way to New Jersey. It was a great day for driving. We made it without incident.

It has now been five years, and we are doing well. Thanks be to God!

Overcoming
Racism
And
Sexism
In the Church

MY FAITH HAS MADE ME STRONG!

Racism and sexism are a double-edged sword for Black women. While I knew something was not quite right about the way I was treated when I was growing up, I did not have a name for it. I became aware of the name for this fierce beast back in the early '70s and '80s. As I learned more, I began to behave differently. I used my knowledge and skill to make changes in my environment, particularly in my church. I became very clear about how this "monster" was used very effectively to keep Black women from participating fully in all aspects of leadership of the church. The articles that follow are just a few examples of my effort to make a change.

Taking Our Place As Black Women In Church Leadership

Not enough women are chairing major committees and boards in our churches. We are seen as a helper, supporters, and too fragile to "hold up" under pressure. We can prepare the communion tray but are too "weak" to carry that heavy tray down the aisle. We earn and pay money to the church, and we manage our own household, sometimes alone, but we are not knowledgeable enough to chair the trustee committee. When it comes to bake sales and dinners, and hosting the coffee hour, who should be asked? Who is at the top of the list to teach Sunday school, and provide nurturing for the in-firmed, yet we who are so capable of mending broken hearts are incapable of carrying "the Word" or sharing "the Word" in the pulpit. At business meetings, we are most often asked to record the notes because we do it so well. The ideas we generate get turned around and credited to the men who are present, or we may get credit for generating the idea, but "Mr. So & So gets to implement it. We get buried under the shadow of Mr. So & So as Mrs. So & So's wife or Mrs. "his last name." Don't you think it is about time we used our own first name and expressed our own ideas from the position of leader?

Black women have carried the leadership of the Black Church too long under the guise of her male counterpart—husband, brother, father. We have wrestled with the complicated relationships and fought with discouraging ideas behind the scene. We have propped him up on every side. It is about time we appreciate ourselves. Stand up my sisters, and "speak your piece." You have proven over and over again that you are capable and knowledgeable, and "can do it." We need each other—male and female, sisters and brothers. Men don't be afraid
Don't fight us, support us as we have supported you. It is not OK to use us as sex symbols and secretaries and cleaning women. We have the skills, we have the commitment, and we are doing the leadership very well.

In general, women have prepared themselves in a more balanced fashion than men. We have had experience in management and finances that we do not count. We have managed the family for years. We saw to it that everyone had food and clothes and that the bills were paid. We were up during the night nursing and doctoring and after that to mend the broken heart.
Have we not skills? We discount ourselves as being unprepared. Yet we are the most prepared because we have had experience. If it was not at home, it was "on the job." The secretary manages the whole office. She protects "the boss," manages the flow of time and people. She juggles her own feelings for the salvation of "the business." You tell me we cannot manage. Where do you run for nurturing when things get tough? Whose shoulder do you cry on? Is it another man—no. You find the most caring woman you know to dump it all out on. Well, who gives advice when the "walls of Jericho" are falling—she does.

Why are so few women in the church in significant leadership positions? Good question. I suspect there are two answers. 1. Women have not yet appreciated all they know and raised up to demand the respect they so rightly deserve, and 2. Men are thrilled for us to stay where we are because they will not have to compete. Their ego will not have to be shattered, and they will not have to work so hard trying to keep up. It is a difficult place to be in on both sides, but we will overcome victoriously.

My Journey At Lincoln Temple UCC And the National UCC

When we moved to Washington, DC, in 1962, I asked my brother-in-law if he knew of a UCC congregation in the area. He remembered that his cousin, Rev. F.A. Hargett, used to visit Lincoln Congregational Temple when he was in town. Also, our next door neighbors (The Gaskins) were members at Lincoln Temple. So, we visited a few times and soon decided this would be our church home. We took our three young daughters, Yvette(6), Karen(5), and Greta(2) with us to Sunday School and church. We started teaching Sunday School soon after that. The pastor was Rev. Channing Phillips. Since the sanctuary was so crowded, nearly every Sunday, we stayed downstairs. There was "standing room only" in the sanctuary.

As the girls grew older, they began to participate with the youth activities, such as the youth choir, and other group activities for their age. They took the confirmation classes and joined as members.

I served on nearly every board/committee of the church and was chair of the Christian Education Board for several years. We invited Dr. Yvonne Delk to conduct leadership training for our board when she was serving on the national church staff located in Philadelphia.

As I became more aware of gender discrimination in society, and in the church, I began to interrupt the male-dominated leadership at Lincoln. I wanted to serve on the diaconate, but I could not, because the quota of women was filled. When I learned of this, I wrote an amendment to the constitution which changed the quota system so that all members would have equal standing, and I could be elected to serve. In the past, only the men served communion in the sanctuary, and the women made all of the preparation and cleaned up afterward. My amendment changed the whole structure. Now both men and women would help prepare, serve and clean up. I was one of the first three women to be ordained as a deacon (Minnie Davis and Verna Robinson were the other two). I was the very first woman to serve communion in the sanctuary. My family came for the ordination and took me out for lunch afterward. Women of the church were incredibly supportive and proud of my action. Not only did I interrupt the diaconate, but I also grabbed Ruth Washington, and we crashed the all-male Usher Board meeting one Sunday making us the first two women to serve on the usher board, previously all male.

Another significant activity was the organizing of a Leadership Development Team. This team included representatives from all of the boards including the Church Council and some ad hoc members. The purpose of this team was to strengthen the boards and support the pastor in ways broader than the church council. I organized a church-wide retreat one year. The theme was "Look Back, Leap Forward." It was a two-day retreat and very well attended. It was held at a local Junior College. Many good things were implemented from that retreat. (The pastor then was Rev. Benjamin E. Lewis).

I organized a banner committee. We made banners for significant seasons of the Christian year and other occasions. Some of those banners are still being used. I was an officer of the Women's Fellowship and president of the Pacesetters club.

As I grew in confidence and knowledge of the wider church, I began to serve on various association and conference committees. The first association committee I served was the Potomac Association Christian Education. I moved on to others including the Conference Board of Directors, and The Church and Ministry Committee of the Association. I served as the Associate Moderator of the Potomac Association. In 1977, I was elected as a delegate from the Central

Atlantic Conference (CAC) to the General Synod. The General Synod was held in Washington, DC, that year.

At that General Synod, I was elected President of the Black Women's Caucus of United Black Christians (UBC). Many of the women of Lincoln Temple were at that meeting and supported me wholeheartedly. As a result of my leadership in UBC, I noticed a significant void in the leadership of Black Women throughout the church, but particularly at the national setting. I was determined to do something to change that reality. I developed a model leadership development program to train and empower Black women in how the "decision making" process of the UCC worked. The project was named "Empowerment for Change.
(Read the story elsewhere in these writings.)

While serving as a delegate of the CAC, I went on to serve on other boards at the national setting. The OCIS, CCW, OCLL, and BHM. I was voted one of the outstanding women by CCW and was elected alternate chairperson of the Biennial Women's Conference. I attended the first National Women's Conference in Cincinnati, OH. I was chosen to visit Germany to a "Just Peace" conference with a team from OCIS. I went to Zimbabwe to the pre-World Council of Churches closing of the Decade of Churches in Solidarity with Women. Deborah E. Braden and I traveled together with a group and were roommates at that conference together. I was secretary of the national UBC for a few years and helped organize a chapter in Region III which includes the Central Atlantic Conference. I also served as president of Region III for a few years.

I am blessed to have known and served with some of the "giants" of the UCC. As I write this reflection, I am thinking of more and more stories that have enriched my journey.

CAC—Central Atlantic Conference   CCW—Coordinating Center for Women
OCIS—Office for Church in Society   OCLL—Office for Church Life and Leadership
BHM – Board for Home Land Ministries UBC—United Black Christians

Empowerment For Change —The Story

When our family settled in Washington, DC, we established a church home at Lincoln Temple UCC. Right away both my husband and I began helping in the church school. I taught kindergarten and primary classes for several years. I served on the Board of Christian Education as a member, and as chairperson, developing innovative and creative ways to work with the total educational program of the church. I was given many opportunities to "stretch and grow."

I served the Potomac Association as a member of the Christian Education Committee and as Associate Moderator. I served on the Central Atlantic Conference Board of Directors, and the Consultant Services Network. I was elected delegate to the General Synod in 1977 (the bi-annual decision-making body of the denomination) and was elected President of the Black Women's Caucus at that meeting. This was the first national office I had ever held. After that, I went on to serve on other boards and committees. I served six years on the Directorate of the Office for Church in Society (OCIS), and liaison to the Coordinating Center for Women (CCW)...seven years on the Directorate of the Office for Church Life and Leadership (OCLL), and liaison to the Coordinating Center for Women, where I was Associate Moderator for the Second Biennial Assembly. I served on the Human Sexuality project for the United Church Board for Homeland Ministries (BHM), and I served as Secretary of the National United Black Christians (UBC). I learned a lot from those experiences. I became aware of the lack of Black women in the decision-making process of the church.

In early January I took a training lab with the National Training Leadership Institute (NTL) on becoming a change agent. I left that event before it was over to join the first National UCC Women's Conference In Cincinnati, OH (January 10-13, 1979) when I returned home highly motivated (revved up). I could hear the "Spirit of God" speaking to me, and directing me to develop a plan to get more Black women in leadership beyond the local church.

On that next Sunday, I spoke with a member of my church who had knowledge about resources in the Potomac Association. I shared my vision and asked for help. We met for brunch and a brainstorming session. He liked the idea and agreed to help develop a plan to train three or four Black women as consultants with two as members of the steering committee of the Black Women's Caucus. My friend wrote to the appropriate committee chairperson of the Potomac Association asking for funding and next steps. The chairperson agreed to work with us. He wrote to all of the churches in the Central Atlantic Conference (CAC) asking for volunteers. Six volunteers decided to take the training. The training was in Human Relations and Leadership Development with the Mid-Atlantic Training and Consultants Network (MATC), and the National Training Lab (NTL). We used all of the budget allocated for training for that year.

Another appeal was made to the Chairperson of the Parish Services Committee (PSC). He responded indicating a need to meet and discuss next steps. I asked the moderator of my local church (Lincoln Temple UCC) to attend the meeting with me. I kept praying and asking God for wisdom and direction. In that meeting, we developed a draft program outline and a budget for implementation. The draft included submitting a proposal to several national agencies for funding, organize an opening event in September, followed by a two-year intensive training for ten women from the CAC churches. I could not move fast enough. I felt like I was "chasing my shadow" so-to-speak. Deadlines were short.

I went to work on the proposal immediately. With the help of a friend, I was able to submit a draft proposal by the deadline. When I heard the committee had accepted and would sponsor the project, I was both thrilled with excitement and overcome with fear. "What do I do now? Can I do this? What have I gotten myself into?" I used the tools of Re-Evaluation Counseling to help me work through that fear and keep moving. Fortunately, a member of the PSC was assigned to work with me, as a consultant.

Oddly enough, all of the people in leadership who had helped me get to this point were men. However, they were very supportive and helped to move the project along. When I met with my PSC consultant for the first time, we focused on things that must be completed by the September 14-15 deadline. We agreed the first thing needed was a flyer introducing the project to the CAC delegates to the General Synod meeting June 20-27, 1979. To produce the flyer we needed a date, place, speaker and a theme. My consultant worked on the flyer, while I worked frantically on getting a place and speaker confirmed. On June 11, the moderator of Lincoln Temple, the PSC consultant and I met and worked out a theme. The flyer was ready the day before I left for the 12th General Synod held in Indianapolis, IA. I talked with the CAC delegates and distributed flyers for information back home.

The project for training Black women was named, "Empowerment for Change." The goals of the project were:

to provide opportunities for basic skills in leadership development;

to establish communication channels for information sharing;

to gather Black women periodically for building mutual sharing and resource development; and

to hear, witness and minister in the spirit of Christ.

While I worked on submitting the proposal for funding of the project to several National UCC agencies, my PSC consultant worked on a contract with Mid Atlantic Training and Consulting (MATC). I made a personal appeal to each agency contact via telephone followed by a copy of the proposal. Each agency needed an endorsement from the conference minister, and a statement from me indicating how the leadership training would be used in society.

On July 9th, my PSC consultant and I met. He introduced the project to the MATC staff. One of the Black women consultants (Dr. Bessie Howard) of the MATC staff volunteered to work with me. Bess and I met for the first time on July 16th. We had lunch and chatted about how she would support me. She agreed to help design the September event and actually lead the Friday activities. She also decided to work with the project until it was finished, without charge. Wow, this was mind-boggling. I could not believe this miracle, but it was true. Dr. Yvonne Delk was the keynote speaker. She led a superb presentation on the decision-making process of the UCC. The event was highly successful

Copies of the proposal were mailed to all pastors of predominantly Black congregations in the CAC with a plea for support. These letters were sent on September 6th. I met and personally interviewed each of these pastors. The purpose of the interview was to explain the project, answer any questions, and solicit support both for the project and the participants.

The first support group meeting was October 13th. There were eight women present. We spent most of the time talking about the schedule and clarifying questions about the project. Each woman was asked to talk about her expectations from the project. I worked really hard between October 13th and November 3rd (the first training event) to bring the number of participants up to ten. There were seven committed women present on November 3rd. I had to "keep the faith," "pray without ceasing," and keep focused. There was a lot of work associated with moving the project along, but the dividends were great.

Each support group was focused on a different aspect of the church, and the decision-making process in that arena. For example, the second support group meeting was focused on the decision making process in the CAC. The conference minister gave the presentation.

The project was designed to cover two years, with recruitment targeted at crucial parishes throughout the conference. Our goals were accomplished. Eight women completed the project. Our presence made a significant impact in the church. All of us moved into significant leadership positions easily at all settings of the church. The project was a huge success. Thanks be to God!

For further information contact:
Yvonne Marrow, Coordinator
Lincoln Congregational Temple
1701 11th Street, N.W.
Washington, D.C. 20001
Telephone: (202) 332-2640

This report was funded by the United Church of Christ, Commission for Racial Justice

SPONSORED BY:
PARISH SERVICES COMMITTEE
CENTRAL ATLANTIC CONFERENCE
SILVER SPRING, MARYLAND

My Journey To Zimbabwe

My journey to Zimbabwe to attend the World Council of Churches closing Festival of the Ecumenical Decade of Churches in Solidarity with Women, started long before I realized I would actually get to go. I saw an article in the "Common Lot" (the women's magazine of the UCC) that caught my attention. The article mentioned groups making quilts as gifts for the participants at the closing festival of the Ecumenical Decade of Churches in Solidarity with Women. I thought it was a great idea, so I brought the idea to the meeting of the Women's Fellowship of Lincoln Temple (my home church) for their support.

A small group of women, primarily first-time quilters, volunteered to participate. The project evolved into an exciting adventure. Some of the women worked on their quilt exclusively in their homes, while others met at the church weekly. I visited with one woman, in her home, every week until her quilt was finished. Altogether, the group completed 26 quilts and prepared a dedication service in conjunction with the Women's Day service that year.

We gave eight quilts to the Chi Child Care Center—a Border Baby House, we sent 16 to New York to be shipped to Zimbabwe, and we kept two to begin our project for the sick and shut-ins of Lincoln Temple as Christmas gifts.

While I was attending a board meeting of the Coordinating Center for Women (CCW), I let it be known that I was interested in going to the Decade Festival. To my surprise, someone negotiated for me to go as a regional representative to the Festival.

Participants had to finance their own way, so I asked the Women's Fellowship to sponsor a fundraising raffle to help me. I made a quilt specifically for the raffle. Between the raffle and contributions from family, friends and other churches, we raised sufficient funds to claim my blessing.

The excitement began to build. I made sure to get the necessary shots and medical supplies. I bought a camcorder. The salesperson gave me a crash course, and I had a few days to practice. I borrowed an electrical adapter from a church friend.

After gathering all of the things I needed for my trip, I spread everything on my bed. I slept on the couch because I did not want to move anything. I planned a "packing party" so I would not be alone. Several family members came and brought food. I prepared a checklist so I would be sure to carry everything I needed.

Deborah Brayton of New York and I were all set to be traveling partners. My daughter Karen took me to the airport in Washington, DC, and waited until my plane took off. After landing at LaGuardia, NY, I met Deborah at her church as planned. She took me to her house where she finished packing and took care of other arrangements before leaving for Kennedy airport. We had a stopover in London where we met other delegates to the Festival. We met a woman from Victoria Toa home of Victoria Falls.

After we got checked in at the Belvedere Technical Teachers College, our home for the Festival in Zimbabwe, we went to the Eastgate Shopping Center to exchange money, and arrange our tour to Victoria Falls. We were up early the next morning on our way to the airport. The Breakaway Safari van was waiting for us when we arrived in Victoria Falls. We traveled to the office where we mapped out our day. We took the guided tour of the Falls, had lunch on the Zambezi River, a tour of the traditional village, and some shopping. The Falls were awesome. Our driver took us past the Baobab Tree, said to be about 114 years old. There were nine of us on the boat for lunch. The chef prepared an excellent meal. He provided some historical information while we sailed. We saw two families of hippos, elephants, a crocodile, and all kinds of birds in the water and on the banks of the river.

The Festival was international. I met women from Chili, Pakistan, Ethiopia, and many other countries. It was an awesome feeling to reach out and touch sisters from around the world. The Festival was informative, exhilarating and there was so much to learn. There were lots of workshops, dancing and singing in other languages. The US delegates met daily to debrief, and plan our participation.

Our return was a bit challenging since there came a storm which grounded our scheduled plane. We had to spend an extra night, but our traveling partners were creative in making arrangements for us to get a flight out via South Africa.

Air travel for this trip was most unusual. I experienced 8 airports—Reagan National, Washington, DC; LaGuardia & Kennedy in New York; Gatwick in London; Harare & Victoria Falls, Zimbabwe; Johannesburg, SA; Cabo Verde Island. And 4 currencies—American Dollar, British Pound, Zimbabwe Dollar, and Rends in South Africa.

Purpose Of Our Family Reunion

To keep the family connected—since our family members live in so many locations, we do not get to visit each other often. So, we are intentional about getting together periodically. If this did not happen, young ones would arrive and grow up without knowing their "next of kin." It is important to know one's family circle.

To perpetuate the family history—It is our custom to prepare a written update—souvenir booklet that contains births, marriages, graduations, significant achievements, and events that have occurred during the previous year. This documentation is crucial for later years when current generations have passed on. The new generations will have a ready record that can be helpful in understanding themselves, and some of the ways their lives have been shaped.

To instill family values—Christian values were modeled and taught by our ancestors and perpetuated in all generations. Most of us were taken to church as young children, and many of us participate in church regularly. We discourage the use of alcohol, illegal drugs, and other substances that are harmful to our bodies and minds. We believe it is important to "treat others as we would like to be treated." Our bodies are a temple.

To promote leadership—Each person is encouraged to reach for their highest potential. To follow the Army slogan—"Be All You Can Be." Set high goals, and reach beyond what is possible. Step out front.

To be trailblazers—We encourage family members to implement their ideas and dreams. Do not wait for someone else to do the things you've dreamed of. Follow your own star. "March to the beat of your own drum." Go for it!

To model good citizenship—A couple of lines from a poem I learned when I was young says, "I soon can learn to do it if you'll let me see it done. I can see your hands in action, but your tongue too fast may run…." We show our young people how a loving family should live. They don't have to ask if they're loved. They know because they see love in action. They see how family members behave with each other.

To provide a safe space—There is so much violence in our society, it is essential to provide a loving family where one can be sure they are loved and respected for who they are. You do not have to "be on guard." You can relax—be yourself. A place where you are excited to bring your friends.

To support each other—We lend a hand whenever there is a need. It can be emotional, financial or physical. We celebrate with each other, pray for healing, actually spend "hands-on" time when necessary.

I Believe in Miracles

On Wednesday, September 1999, Hurricane Floyd was raging in the Atlantic Ocean near the coast of Florida. Meteorologist had predicted this storm to be the worst storm of the decade, even the century. It was predicted that the entire state of Florida could be affected. Folk in that state began a mass exodus, blocking all roads heading north. Traffic was so horrendous the transportation officials changed all highways to lead in the northerly direction. The stories of survival, rescue, and surprise are many from Florida to New Jersey and all along the East Coast.

Why do I include this story? I add this story because I must share the Good News of God's love at every opportunity. Some members of my family were in the direct path of that storm, all the way along the East Coast including myself. While all of us were unharmed, there was much anxiety until the storm had passed entirely. Thank God for cell phones.

Nacole (my granddaughter) was in the Navy and stationed in Florida, Yvette (my daughter)and her sons and grandson were in Dazel, near Sumpter, South Carolina. I had two sisters and other relatives in North Carolina. More family in Virginia, Washington, DC, and Maryland, and me and one daughter and her family here in New Jersey.

The storm did not hit landfall in all of the places that had been predicted, meaning the flooding was not as severe as had been anticipated in some areas. We kept checking on each other as the storm progressed. Flash flooding occurred in many places including here in New Jersey. I have never witnessed "flash flooding" before. What a surprise, and what a miracle. When I reflect on the path of that storm, and the devastation of so many people including the loss of property and lives, I cannot help but praise God in the highest for all the blessings of safety and protection of our family.

HOW CAN THERE BE THOSE WHO BELIEVE THERE IS NO GOD?

Reunion 2019

PLAN TO LIVE FOREVER
Family Reunion-2018

My philosophy for life is "live and let live." I joke about living forever, but "living forever" is really not a joke. I want to be remembered long after I am no longer here in "the flesh." My branches will continue to grow, and my legacy will live on. I am in the process of writing parts of my journey that will be bound and available for people to read, but I want to be remembered by those of you reading this note for the personal impact my journey has made on you.

"Plan to live forever."—Plant your roots in the minds and hearts of others so that something you say or do will "live forever." Age is a gift from God, and it is up to each of us to appreciate and enjoy this gift to the fullest. I cherish the years I have been privileged to enjoy.

My parents planted strong roots. I honor and remember them for the lessons they taught me by word and deed. I respect their legacy. They planted strong roots. We are their branches that keep on growing. I remember vividly some of the specific things I learned by observing their words and actions. I remember how people in the church and community respected them. I remember their generosity and openness, and I especially remember their love for all of us. Whether anyone reading this note knew my parents personally or not, our annual family reunions honor and refresh their legacy. We tell their story in so many different ways throughout the year, and when we gather.

"Plan to live forever."—Some of you will remember when my body was stronger, and I was financially abler, I was there for nearly every family celebration—birthdays, weddings, graduations, baby showers, initial sermons, etc., etc. That is what I call "live while you are living" as my late cousin Evelyn Leaven said.

"Plan to live forever."—I am active at my church, the Senior Center, I do exercise at the gym, I play pinochle, and other table games. I do jigsaw puzzles, play games on my computer, and keep connected via e-mail, and text.

I "Plan to live forever!"

REUNION 55

2019

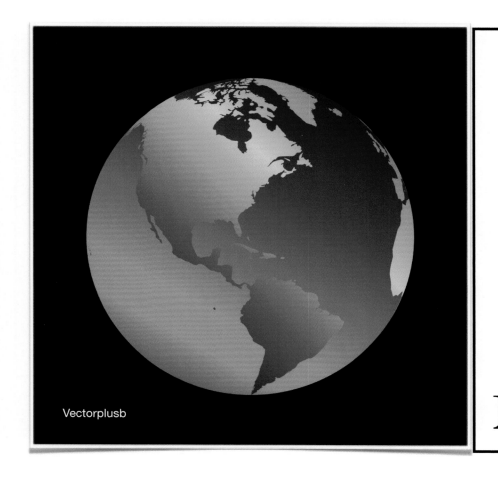

Vectorplusb

A Glimpse of the **World** From a Few of My Visits

While I have visited and seen so many places not documented here, these are just a few that will give a flavor of my travel over the years. I have traveled for pleasure, for business, and for my church. I have traveled alone, with friends and with family. I have traveled by automobile, train, plane and a ship on the ocean. There are no limits to the memories I have stored from my glimpse from other parts of the globe.

ASIA

Daria Andrianova

Holy Land

Israel

Jordan

Been There! – Done That!

From the farmland to the Holy Land;
From the outhouse to the White House;
From the mule and wagon to the Boeing 747;
From rain falling off the housetop to Victoria Falls in Africa;
From the pig path to the TurnPike;
From the sweet potato bank to the Pyramids in Egypt;
From being baptized in the Black Swamp Creek
To being baptized in the Jordan River and
From the homeland to the Motherland.

Yes, I have been there and done that! Had I not moved or relocated so many times, there is no way my eyes could have seen, my ears could have heard, or my body experienced so many wonderful things. I have met so many great people along the way—from the homeless to people with distinguished titles. God has blessed me with good health, and keeps right on blessing me every day. I am so thankful.

The Middle East

My Pilgrimage To The Land Of The Bible

My God is an awesome God
God reigns from heaven above
With wisdom, power, and love
My God is an awesome God.

These words became the theme song for many as we rode miles of rocky desert and trekked to the top of numerous mountains overlooking fertile valleys, and crossed over bodies of water I thought I would only read about. Shepherds stood by their sheep and goats grazed on the mountainside as camels
roamed free.

We observed the quiet streets of Jerusalem on the Sabbath and the noisy, busy streets of Egypt in the overcrowded metropolis of Cairo on the Nile. We heard the Moslem's call to prayer from a high tower and visited their mosque where we took off our shoes to enter. We walked the Via Dolorosa in the pouring rain—the route Jesus took the cross.

We went through border controls as we passed from one country to another, and observed different cultures at their everyday living.

The Bible literally came alive as we walked where Jesus walked, saw where He was born, grew up, was imprisoned, crucified, arose, and ascended to heaven. Although many of the sites were traditional (not proven to be the actual site), the symbolism was enough to prick my imagination and make that portion of the Bible come alive.

I began to appreciate my home in the USA more and more as the people in the streets were begging at every stop. Some of the living conditions were extreme. Many people, called Bedouins, lived in mud and goat-skin huts and caves on the mountainside, the rocky desert valleys, and along the river Nile, while others lived in palatial palaces surrounded by lots of land, expensive automobiles, and manicured lawns.

There were 25 in our group. We lived in all five-star hotels with plenty of food served buffet style. We had lunch at Class A restaurants in the tour areas and had absolutely superb tour guides.

There are no words to describe some of our experiences. The only way to truly grasp the reality of this blessed country is to be there.

I count it a privilege and a blessing to have been on this tour at this time in my life.

The Pilgrimage

All of the events of the Bible took place in that part of the world known as the Middle East—the territory that lies north, south, and east of the Mediterranean Sea. The Middle East holds a key position as a crossroads between three continents—Africa, Asia, and Europe. There are vast stretches of desert wasteland and uninhabitable mountain ranges.

JORDAN

We flew into Amman, the present-day capital of Jordan. In biblical times, the town called Rabab of the Ammonites. Our first day in Jordan was devoted to visiting Petra known in biblical times as Seri. This Old Testament town was home of the Edomite's at the time of the Exodus. The only entrance into this fortress city is through a narrow canyon that opens up into larger canyons. Its sandstone sculptured walls still stand full of splendor, grandeur, and eloquence as if carved with modern-day tools.

Our tour guide pointed out aqueducts carved out of the solid rock on each side of the winding path which had brought water to the ancient city. He also helped us visualize the people and their activities as they must have lived "in those days."

Our tour continued the next day with a climb of Mt. Nebo where we stood on the top of Pisgah, the place where God showed Moses the Promised Land but did not allow him to cross over into it because of his unfaithfulness toward God.

We saw a place believed to be the site where God destroyed Sodom and Gomorrah. We stopped to pick up rocks and take pictures. We continued to Jeresh for lunch and a look at the ruins of the Roman Provincial city, its temples, theaters, and colonnades. Jeresh was a center of trade from the earliest times. We stopped to touch the rock, and the stream believed to be the rock struck by Moses. Later that day, we drove along the Peace Highway and across the Jordan River into Israel. After checking through customs, we met our new tour guide and the bus driver who took us to our hotel.

ISRAEL

During the life and ministry of Jesus, the Roman Empire controlled the nation of Israel. The area was so large that it became an administrative problem for the Roman government. Thus, the Roman Emperor divided the territory. The land of Palestine was the central part of the country and Judea in the south. The following are some of the places we visited.

Bethlehem, called Ephrata in biblical times, is located in the province of Judea and stands five miles south of Jerusalem. It was mentioned in the Bible in connection with the death of Rachel. There is a small dome monument over her tomb. It is sacred to Jews, Moslems, and Christians. Women of the area visit and pray for successful childbirth. Ruth and Boaz met and married, and David was born and anointed King of Israel by the Prophet Samuel.

The birth of Jesus in Bethlehem rendered this little town immortal and made its name live in the hearts of Christians for over 2000 years.

The Church of the Nativity is the oldest church in the Holy Land and probably the oldest in the world. The entrance was lowered twice to prevent Moslem invaders from entering on horseback.

The entrance leads to the cave which has a silver star that marks the spot where Christ was born. The manger which lies to the right was probably used for storing hay. It was the best and driest spot to place the baby.

Nazareth is one of the leading Christian cities. It is the place where Jesus grew to manhood. When He began to minister, He was not understood here. After the first attempt was made on His life, Jesus left Nazareth, went down to Capernaum and made it His city.

Capernaum is located 2.5 miles from where the Jordan River enters the Sea of Galilee. At the time of Jesus, it was probably the largest and richest city along the shores of the sea with a customs station and a residence for high Roman officers. Here, Jesus taught in the synagogue, healed the leper, delivered a man of unclean spirit, healed Peter's mother-in-law, healed the woman with the issue of blood, healed the blind men, healed the withered hand and much more. Jesus pronounced a curse on the city of Capernaum. The prophecy was fulfilled, and the city was destroyed and the site lost for a long time. Today, Capernaum is no more than a heap of ruins in the midst of palms beside the lake.

Mary's Well is one of the authentic sites in the Holy Land. It was, and still is, the city's only water supply. The Greek Orthodox claim that the Annunciation took placed while Mary was drawing water from the fountain and they built their church over it.

Cana lies 4 miles along the road from Nazareth to Tiberius. There are three or four places of that name, but this one is most favored. Cana is known throughout the whole Christian world as the scene of Jesus' first miracle—He changed water into wine at the wedding feast.

Tiberius lies 682 feet below sea-level on the west side of the Sea of Galilee. It is the most popular winter resort in Israel. At the time of Jesus, Galilee was the main artery of road crossing in all directions. Here is where Jesus began His public ministry—teaching and preaching and performing miracles. He called His apostles here on the shore of the sea. He spoke to the multitude from Peter's boat, commanded the violent storm to be still, and walked on the stormy water.

Overlooking the Sea of Galilee is an octagonally shaped chapel situated atop the **Mount of Beatitudes** marking the spot where Jesus delivered the Sermon on the Mount. On each window of the cupola is written part of the text of the eight Beatitudes.

Jericho has been well-known for the richness of its well-watered soil and its oranges, bananas, and dates. Traveling back to Jerusalem, Jesus passed through Jericho. Amongst the crowd of people waiting to catch a glimpse of Him was a small man named Zacchaeus. It was called the city of palms and is considered the oldest city in the world to have been discovered so far.

The **Jordan** is a holy river. It twists and curves in a 160-mile long bed, while the distance it covers is only 65 miles in a straight line. Its width is 100 feet. Jesus came from Galilee and was baptized in the River Jordan by St. John. The traditional spot where Jesus was baptized is located 5 miles east of Jericho. Five of us were baptized during a service there.

The temptation of Jesus was immediately after his baptism in the Jordan River. Neither the Gospel nor any other source enables us to determine precisely the spot where Jesus underwent His forty days of fasting. Later tradition indicated the Mount of Qarantal, which rises up behind the old Jericho, as the site of the first and third temptations. At the top of the mountain are the remains of the chapel which marks the spot where satan tempted Jesus. This mountain is called Mt. Temptation.

The Dead Sea is 47 miles long and 10 miles wide. The Dead Sea lies 1,200 feet below sea level, which is the lowest spot on the earth's surface. It is called the Dead Sea because no animal life is in its water. It is the most salt-saturated water in the world. The reason why the Dead Sea is a high concentration of chemicals is that it has no outlet.

About 2 ½ miles from the western shore of the Dead Sea, in the wilderness of Judea, stands the rock fortress of Masada. Herod the Great built a huge magnificent fortress at the top of Masada. After the destruction of Jerusalem in 70 A.D., a band of Jewish patriots marched on Masada and captured it from a Roman garrison. After a long siege of many months of hard fighting, the Jewish patriots, realizing that it was impossible to hold out any longer, the 967 defenders committed suicide, preferring to die as free men rather than be taken into captivity by the Romans. The Romans entered the fortress, saw the bodies, and heard the story from the two women who, with five small children, had hidden themselves.

Jerusalem is the sacred city of half the human race since it is the religious capital of three major faiths—for the Jews, it is the symbol of their past glories and the hope of their future. For the Christians, it is the city of Jesus' last ministry, the city which saw Jesus die on the cross and rise from the dead. For the Moslems, it is the city where the Prophet Mohammed is believed to have ascended into heaven.

Few cities have survived as long as Jerusalem. King David established Jerusalem as the capital of his kingdom about 1000 B.C. after taking the city from a tribal people known as the Jebusites. While the city has grown and changed over the years, it has remained primarily the same site as the very first "city of David" from the nation's past.

The Mount of Olives is located east of Jerusalem across the Kidron Valley. It is the mount where Christ ascended into heaven, foretold the destruction of Jerusalem, taught the Lord's Prayer to His disciples, and often came for meditation and prayer.

The Garden of Gethsemane lies at the foot of the Mount of Olives. This is the garden where Jesus underwent the most sorrowful hour of His passion, choosing to suffer and die on the cross, taking upon Himself the sins of all humankind.

In the memorable Garden of Gethsemane, there are eight olive trees whose age is lost in antiquity. Some botanist claim that they may be 3,000 years old. The olive tree does not die.

The **Kidron Valley** was crossed many times by Jesus either going to the Temple through the Golden Gate or ascending to the Mount of Olives where he used to spend the night. He surely crossed this valley on the memorable evening of Holy Thursday, when he went with his disciples to Gethsemane, and again, after he was betrayed and led to the High Priest Caiaphas.

The church, St. Peter in Gallicantu, was built over the traditional site of the house of the High Priest Caiaphas. Here, Jesus spent the night, and here was the scene of his first trial. St. Peter wept at the crowing of the cock in fulfillment of Christ's words.

Via Dolorosa is the traditional pathway Jesus followed carrying the cross and the events that took place on the way to the crucifixion. There are 14 stations of the cross. Five are inside the Church of the Holy Sepulcher.

The Church of the Holy Sepulchre stands over Golgotha, the place of the Crucifixion, and the tomb where the body of Jesus was laid.

Calvary was a large rock rising about 45 feet out of the ground. Its name (Place of the Skull) probably came from its appearance, which resembles a skull.

The Golden Gate is situated on the site of the original Eastern Gate of the Temple Compound. According to Christian tradition, Jesus passed through this gate when entering Jerusalem with His Disciples on Palm Sunday. The Gate was walled entirely up in 1530 by the Turks.

The Citadel is one of the most well-known landmarks of Jerusalem. It was once the fortress that guarded Herod's Palace. Today the Museum of the City of Jerusalem is located inside the Citadel and exhibitions are held frequently.

The Dome of the Rock, also known as the Mosque of Omar, was built at the end of the 7th century. The Mosque is the oldest and the most exquisite Moslem shrine in the world. The dome, made of a special aluminum bronze ally, shines like gold under the brilliant sun of Jerusalem.

The Western Wall is a portion of the wall that Herod built around the second Temple in 20 B.C. This is the holiest shrine of the Jewish world. It is served as the last relic of the last Temple. Titus, in the year 70 A.D., spared this part of the wall with its huge blocks to show future generations the greatness of the Roman soldiers who had been able to destroy the rest of the building. During the Roman period, Jews were not allowed to come to Jerusalem. However, during the Byzantine period, they were allowed to come over once a year, on the anniversary of the destruction of the Temple, to lament the dispersion of their people and weep over the ruins of the Holy Temple, which is why this section of the wall became known as the Wailing Wall.

Haifa, a little town of 10,000 in 1905, is now the third largest city in Israel with a population of 225,000. It possesses the country's main port and the nation's largest and heaviest industries. It is situated in the most beautiful bay of the Mediterranean coast, and slopes of the most charming mountain in Israel, which is Mt. Carmel. The prophet Elijah confronted the priest of Baal and confronted them when their incantations failed, and his own drew fire from heaven. The Bahia faith considers Haifa as their holy city.

EGYPT

We traveled one whole day from Jerusalem through the Sinai and across the Suez Canal to reach Cairo, Egypt.

The Egyptians gave us VIP service. Not only did we have a police escort all the way from the Israeli border into Cairo, when our tour guide flashed her warm smile and said, "Welcome Home" we knew we could relax and get ready for a great visit.

Cairo is a city of contrasts—ultra-modern apartment buildings next to centuries-old Mosques, narrow stone-paved alleyways abutting superhighways, the homes of the rich not far from the hovels of the poor. Glittering new stores display the latest fashions from Paris and New York. A few minutes away in the bazaar of the Old Quarters, antiquated cubicles offer tapestries, exotic perfumes from Africa, strange confections, hand wrought leathers, and jewelry with designs dating back to the days of the pharaohs. Cairo's skyline is punctuated by the spires of hundreds of towers of the Muslim's Mosques. Two of the prominent features that shape the character of Cairo are the Nile River that runs through the western portion of the city and is alive with shipping much of the time, and the other is the citadel to the southeast. The medieval section of the city is known as Grand Cairo. It lies in the shadow of the Citadel, evidence that the impressive walled city was once the heart of Cairo.

Cairo is built on the banks of the Nile River. As we drove along the river's edge in the nearby countryside on our way to Memphis, we observed the nomadic Bedouin tents and saw people tending their crops. We saw both ancient and modern irrigation systems, and people carrying sugarcane and other harvests to market on camels and trucks, and carts pulled by water buffalo. Memphis is located about twenty miles southwest of Cairo and was one of the most important cities throughout the history of ancient Egypt.

Menes, the first pharaoh of this dynasty, built a vast, white-walled palace and the Temple of Ptah here. During the 950 years of this era, the Egyptians accomplished some remarkable feats. These include the building of the great Pyramids, the invention of paper, and the method of mummifying the dead. They perfected an early system of writing called hieroglyphics that consisted of tiny pictures and symbols.

Sakkara is one of the most exciting historical and archeological areas in all of Egypt. The site, about 12 miles southwest of Cairo, is dominated by the famous Step Pyramid of King Zoser, built during the Third Dynasty of Pharaonic architect, Imhotep. It was the first pyramid to be built in ancient Egypt and was the model for all others. Deep inside this mighty structure was a burial shaft and tomb chambers. As building progressed, other chambers were added to accommodate members of the royal family and space to store clothing, equipment, food and other items needed in the next world. The designers and builders had to be very clever. They built false doors, concealed entrances, and special locks so that would-be thieves could not find certain corridors or the chambers housing the possessions of the departed pharaohs. The ancient robbers were successful so that today, every pyramid in Egypt is empty.

The Egyptian Museum is the most important depository of Egyptian antiquities anywhere in the world. It features artifacts from the Pharaonic and Greco-Roman periods, including the celebrated mummies of ancient Egypt's kings and Tutankhamun treasures. The discovery of King Tutankhamun's tomb, just as it had been left thousands of years before, was the most spectacular find in the history of archaeology. King Tut, was king of all Egypt when he was only nine years old, and died at the age of eighteen.

The Great Pyramids of Giza stands not far from Cairo. More than two million stone blocks weighing an average of 2 ½ tons were used to build this gigantic structure. This pyramid is especially interesting, since its interior burial chambers are open for inspection by the public, and could be seen from our hotel.

Not far from the pyramids is the Great Sphinx of Gaza, which dates back to 2620 B.C. This massive structure is hewn from natural yellowish limestone and standing 65 feet high and 187 feet long, this impressive statue combines the head of a pharaoh with a lion's body.

Our visit to Egypt came at the end of our 13-day tour. We visited many fascinating and magnificent monuments in this birthplace of the oldest civilization in history. I am still sorting out and trying to put everything into perspectives.

I thank God for a rich, safe journey to the HOMELAND.

Dome of the Rock

Baptism in the Jordan

Mount of Beatitudes

MY TRIP TO KENYA, AFRICA

It is impossible to capture in words the experience of wonder and awe I had in Kenya, Africa. This country has poverty and affluence, beauty and splendor, fabulous landscapes and spectacular game reserves. The weather was perfect, and our tour guide was both friendly, and knowledgeable in his area. We traveled bumpy dirt roads and smooth paved roads. We saw all types of animals and birds—large and small including the great wildebeest migration, which included buffalo, zebras, and antelopes (exceeding one million).

We were a party of six—mother and 2 daughters, 1 daughter's husband, 1 niece, and a friend.

A PARTY OF SIX IN AFRICA

It was Saturday, July 21, 2012, when A Party of 6 met at JFK in New York, headed for Kenya, Africa—two from NC—Martha & Delilah, one from MI— Arnese, one from N. J— Greta, and two from Washington, DC—Karen & Ricky.

We generated lots of excitement waiting for each other to get checked thru customs and thru the gate for departure at LaGuardia, NY. Just about midnight that Saturday, we boarded the Turkish Airline headed to Istanbul, Turkey. We had a two-hour layover. We changed planes then continued on to Nairobi, Kenya. We met our Friendly Planet representative who was waiting with a sign. Four other people traveling with the same agency joined our group making 10. All 10 were off to the Intercontinental Hotel in Nairobi for a briefing, a safari hat, and a package of material needed for the rest of our journey.

Words are inadequate to describe the experience of this "jammed packed"8-day schedule. We took so many photos our memories will remain fresh each time we take a look. The first tours included the Daphne Sheldrick Elephant Orphans' Nursery, the Langata Giraffe Center, the Kazuri Bead factory, and the Karen Blixen Museum. We traveled thru the Great Rift Valley to the Lake Naivasha Lodge. After dinner, our group went on a water safari on the lake in several small boats where we saw many species of birds, as well as hippos, gazelles, antelopes and lots of other wildlife along the lake shores.

After a good night's rest, we traveled the long, winding, dusty roads (full of bumps & dips--about five hours), to the Masai Mara Game Reserve. I thought of Black Swamp—back in the day before paved roads. There were shepherds along the hillside with their flock which reminded me of Bible stories I've read. The Masai Mara people greeted us with dancing and native music. I found this to be spectacular. Polygamy is the norm in this culture. At this particular location, there was one man with 13 wives. Each wife had her own hut, which she built with cow dung and urine. There's no way to tell it all. This experience made me really, really appreciate the USA, and my little apartment back home.

Our daily safari tours were exceptional, probably because of our superb driver—he was knowledgable and experienced, and he made sure we were taken to the best sites, to get the best pictures. He shared information that was very helpful to our understanding and experience.

We saw the "Big Five"—the Lion, Elephant, Leopard, Rhino, and the Hippo, as well as many other animals. We were there at the height of the Great Migration of the Wildebeest—the most massive movement of land mammals on the planet. This indescribable scene is probably

Africa's greatest wildlife spectacle and one of the world's most exceptional natural phenomena. Imagine millions of wildebeest mixed with zebras and antelopes, etc. The lions and crocodiles were waiting for a feast, and feast they did. Evidence showed when we saw swarms of vultures hovering over the carcasses left.

On our last night in Nairobi, we were taken to a lovely restaurant where an assortment of wildlife was on the menu, along with great American food.

The trip was almost surreal. We covered so much territory in a short period. While I was exhausted and ready to get home, I wanted to see more and more. We landed back at JFK on Saturday, July 28, 2012. It was like an oasis in my memory. I can go there and enjoy it anytime. It was fabulous, and I recommend it to everyone.

JOHN F. KENNEDY INTERNATIONAL AIRPORT (JFK)

JFK International airport is the US 6th busiest airport and was originally built in 1948 renamed for the slain American President in December 1963. Operated by the Port Authority of New York and New Jersey, JFK airport is located in the borough of Queens only 15 miles from midtown Manhattan. JFK has 8 operating terminals with 125 gates serving over 70 airlines. After a1.4 billion dollar redevelopment in 2001, terminal 4 serves international passengers with the airport's only 24-hour Customs and Border Protection and has the airport's only internal Air Train station to take passengers to the Long Island Rail Road and NYC subway, making for easy access to major corporations and tourist designations. New York entertainment includes TV, music, and 9 major sports teams. Whether dining at one of 12,000 plus restaurants, strolling around 843 acre Central Park or shopping on fashionable 5th avenue, NYC has something for everyone.

PARIS AND LONDON

T'WAS A TRIP OFF TO EUROPE

T'was a trip off to Europe, with a party of six.
A designer, her family, and three aunts in the mix.

Our suitcases were packed, and travel documents gathered with care,
in hopes that everything we needed for the trip would be there.

With luggage checked in, and our seats assigned,
we were most delighted to get out of line.

Around the corner we took a few snaps.
Then we sat and waited for the time to elapse.

We said our goodbyes, crossed the field to the plane.
Waved to the relatives again and again.

Away down the aisles we went straight to our seats.
Fastened our seat belts, and enjoyed the treats.

We arrived at the Charles de Gaulle airport in France on time.
We traipsed through the airport, and waited for our baggage in the line.

Then what to our tuned in ears do you suppose we could hear?
Only French speaking people so very, very near.

With a little knowledge of French, and a few gestures of the hand,
I knew we would make it, and we would understand.

Now, we had to hurry and buy a ticket for the train.
And to make sure we were all there someone shouted out our names.
Where's Etta and Thelma? Yvonne and Caletha are you near?
Come Clarence and Caretha, the train is here.

On the subway we dashed so fast and so bold,
dragging many pieces of luggage right through the door.

We rode and rode 'till we came to our stop.
We jumped off the train, and rushed to the top.

Well folks, let's get a taxi, and find our place to stay.
With a few little obstacles, we finally found our way.

And then in slow motion the elevator came.
T'was small, but it carried our luggage just the same.

Shortly after we entered the room and was doing around,
Sister Etta dropped on the bed that seemed as low as the ground.

She dressed in her nightie for a quick little nap,
while Thelma and Yvonne began to rap.

We unpacked our bags, and hung up our clothes,
and thought we'd better get organized before we began to doze.

Now, we went out to change our money, and get something to eat.
It was a long way for those of us who had corns and bunions on our feet.

We just strolled along taking in the sights,
and some of them were a sheer delight.

The city of Paris is really grand.
Since our French was limited, we communicated through other ways
they would understand.

We were so clumsy, and awkward at times.
We laughed at ourselves, and hoped the French people didn't mind.

Now, it was time to prepare for the International Trade Show,
And away across town on the subway Caretha and Yvonne had to go.

We went straight to her booth in that very large hall.
She found her sponsor, and they displayed her designs on the walls.
They were so beautifully arranged, it made us stand tall.

With everything in order for the buyers to see,
they stood with amazement in awe and did agree.
"You have something unique, very beautiful indeed.
I'll sell in my country, I'll take an order."
They were excited, and full of glee.

Some days the aisles were so full one could hardly walk,
and the place was buzzing, as you could hear everyone talk.

When the show was over and the buyers gone,
we packed up our wares, and made our way home.

Now we visited two European cities on this trip with six.
Getting to London was quite a trick.

We rode on taxies, and two different trains.
We rode on a Hovercraft on and off again.

No language barriers in this city to cause us stress,
but it was the money conversion—the dollar was less.

London is a city of royalty indeed.
We visited some of the popular tourist places.
Since we couldn't see them all,
we'll have to check out books from the library and read.

The underground transport system was really great.
We rode it to all the places we ate.

We visited the royal palace, and saw the changing of the guards.
We even went shopping in the most famous
department store in London—Harrod's.

We went to see a comedy play, and laughed a lot.
It helped us unwind after a very busy day, and our money's worth we got.

As we boarded the plane, leaving Europe behind,
You could hear each one echo over and over again,
"We had a good time!"

A great big thank you to the Crawford family,
and to all who helped us make the trip joyfully.

MY TRIP TO LAS VEGAS
September 7-11, 2010

This was my first trip to Las Vegas, NV. Greta went out there for a medical conference. Since both of us were celebrating milestone birthdays (Greta 50 and me 80), Karen decided to gift both of us with a fun vacation, and a fun vacation it was. Marie and Yvette took me to the Coastal Carolina Regional Airport in New Bern and waited to see me off. Greta left from Philadelphia, PA. She arrived at the Vegas airport a little before me. We connected by cell phone gathered our bags and caught the last shuttle out to the hotel.

We stayed at THE RED ROCK CASINO, RESORT HOTEL. It is no ordinary Las Vegas destination. It offers the ultimate in resort amenities fused effortlessly with breathtaking views. This billion dollar Resort is nestled at the gateway of the Red Rock National Conservation area in the Northwest Valley. Its 814 rooms and suites have views of either the Red Rock Canyons to the west or a sweeping panoramic view of the Las Vegas Strip to the east.

We stayed in room 10125 (10th floor) on the east with a panoramic view of "The Strip." After Greta checked in for her conference, we went for a quick snack and to try our hand at the Casino. It was fun, but we did not take home THE CASH POT.

The next afternoon we enjoyed an Aroma Therapy Massage, the whirlpool, and the sauna, before going out to dinner. We connected with our cousins Theodore and Gloria Baxter. They were terrific hosts. We had dinner at THE STRATOSPHERE TOWER RESTAURANT. They came and picked us up at the hotel Theodore accompanied us for dinner, but Gloria had a problem with height, so she chauffeured us.

This is a special occasion restaurant located at the top of the Stratosphere Tower and has a spectacular view of the entire valley. It also slowly rotates. The atmosphere is terrific, and the food is fabulous! The service is great. We were seated near the window looking down over the twinkling diamond lights of the strip in all its glory. I had a fabulous lobster meal consisting of two baby lobster tails stuffed with crab meat served over a bed of rice with julienne vegetables on top. Oh so scrumptious! Then, a glass of champagne at the end, to top it off. Yum! Yum! We went to another restaurant another night where Gloria was more comfortable.

They took us for a ride down THE STRIP" after dinner. Las Vegas specializes in over-the-top eye candy. The world famous 4-mile stretch of Las Vegas Boulevard is a glittery, real-life, make-believe world with a replica Brooklyn Bridge, dancing Italian fountains, a lava-spewing volcano an Arthurian castle, pirate ships and a tower that looks like Seattle's Space Needle on steroids. Some of the hotels on the strip are among the world's most mammoth. At night, a phantasmagoria of neon lights blazes bright. A near constant cross-section of humanity shuffles down the sidewalks wandering (and often stumbling) in and out of casinos where dice and wheels 'n reels spin to a soundtrack of joyous shouts, gone bust groans and a cacophony of slot machines blips, beeps, and pings. The bottom line here? "Casinos are King."

On the next night, we went to the theater. We virtually climbed Pride Rock and entered the Circle of Life along with Simba as we took our seats in the orchestra section of the Mandalay Bay Theater to enjoy Disney's "The Lion King." Currently in its twelfth successful year on Broadway and seen by more than 45 million people in 11 countries, Disney's "The Lion King" continues to reign as one of the most popular and beloved shows around the world. With a story that reaches a vast expanse of people regardless of race or culture, The Lion King presents the tale of a lion cub as he journeys into adulthood and faces his royal destiny.

Simba, son of the strong and wise King Mufasa, lives a happy childhood until his evil uncle Scar plots to take over the throne and drives Simba away from the kingdom. In exile, the young cub befriends the hilarious Pumba the warthog and Timon the meerkat and learns their motto of carefree life, "Hakuna Matata." However, as Simba approaches adulthood, he realizes what he has left behind and that he must reclaim his destiny as king of Pride Rock.

The Lion King makes the African savannah come alive through a colorful array of masks and puppets, and the audience will be drawn onto the savannah with them through an exhilarating musical score. Featuring all of Elton John and Tim Rice's songs from the animated film as well as three new songs by the composers, The Lion King fuses Western popular music with the distinctive sounds and rhythms of Africa. From the Academy Award-winning "Can You Feel the Love Tonight" and the haunting "Shadowlands," The Lion King will take you on a touching musical journey.

With plenty of love, laughs, and an amazing soundtrack, The Lion King, is a Disney masterpiece. We enjoyed watching Simba take his place in the Circle of Life. We returned to the hotel in a limousine. Yes, we "lived it up."

Our trip would not have been complete without a trip to M &M WORLD. Yep, it's a tourist trap. Four floors, FOUR FLOORS of nothing but M & M's. The majority is merchandise of the usual style - magnets, key chains, coffee mugs, glasses, figurines, what have you, all of M & M's. The top floor features a cool NASCAR exhibit with Kyle Busch's #18 M & M's stock car on display, and a lot of NASCAR stuff for sale. My favorite part--on the 2nd floor, the wall of M & M's... EVERY color of the rainbow, all in order. You just grab a bag, and you pick what colors you want, or grab the mixed tube if you like. Every type of M & M available, it's there. Greta even got a picture with "Green" on the way in! A great little store... a bit pricey, but well worth it. Greta bought personalized M & M's for Mark and Gabrielle in their favorite colors, in addition to the clothing items. I bought a couple of magnets.

We picked up a few souvenirs at a nearby store, then we waited for Theodore & Gloria to pick us up for dinner at the TUSCANY GARDENS RESTAURANT. It has a cozy, welcoming atmosphere with fabulous food. This 5-star Italian restaurant served delicious cuisine. I had Shrimp Scampi, and Greta had the Halibut. Our cousins were gracious hosts. We enjoyed ourselves tremendously. Theodore made sure we received one of the menu lights as a souvenir. We visited their fabulous home after the meal. Gloria collects elephants, and did she have elephants--unlimited number of ordinary and unusual elephants in lots of colors and different materials—china, crystal, velvet, copper--you name it, she had it. I've never seen so many elephants in one place before in so many different colors and sizes. That was fascinating. They took us back to our hotel, and we bid them farewell.

Well, it is true, all good things must come to an end, and so it did. When we got back to the hotel that night, we packed our bags, went down to drop in a few more coins, hoping to hit the BIG ONE, but it did not happen. We spent down to our last two cents, but did we ever have fun! I can't remember when I have had so much fun before.

We got up early for our trip to the airport and had a light breakfast there. Our flight times were very close. Mine left a little before Greta's. I had a long layover in Atlanta, GA. My friend, Erna Bryant, picked me up, and we went for dinner between flights at the Spondylitis restaurant. Talk about maximizing my time, I did it.
Back home again. Yvette, Marie, and Lonell were waiting for me at Ellis Airport. Since Yvette was driving my car, I just got behind the wheel when they got home and made it home to Jacksonville. AND A GOOD TIME WAS HAD BY ALL!

A SIX CITY TRAIN TRIP

On September 18, 2001, thirty-six enthusiastic Howard University Alumni and friends boarded Train #29—The Capital Limited, for a 17 day trip across country from Washington, DC (the Chocolate City), to visit six cities. From Chicago, IL (The Windy City), to Denver, CO (The Mile High City), and Albuquerque, NM, (Home of the Pueblo Indians). We stopped for a few hours in Raton, NM, just long enough to observe and admire the beautiful mountains and wait for the train that would take us on to El Paso, TX on the Mexican Border. The next stop was San Antonio, TX (Home of the Alamo). From Texas, we went on to New Orleans, LA (Home of the historic French Quarters and the world famous Mardi Gras). We stayed one or two nights in each of these cities and used buses for tours and connections to the next train.

"Doing" the train was quite an experience. All of our connecting trains were off schedule except the one from New Orleans to Washington, DC, at the end of the trip. Amtrak issued a voucher to each of us for a free trip, because we complained. My traveling friend, Merlene Bagley and I decided to take our "free" trip to Canada. So, read all about it on the next page.

MY TRAIN TRIP THROUGH THE PACIFIC NORTHWEST

Brilliant gold and yellow, bright red and brown, even purple dotted the awesome green mountainside. Clouds cascading over snow-capped mountains were breathtakingly beautiful. Now and then there was a stream gurgling over huge boulders making its way to the river. We rode many miles alongside the river's edge with mountains in the distance, and birds were stalking for their prey near the side of the river in the early morning.

We picked the perfect time to travel through the Pacific Northwest.   I can hear that familiar "all aboard" as we were preparing to leave one station on to the next, and the train whistle was blowing as we roared along winding our way toward the next station stop.
It took three days from Washington, DC, to reach Portland, OR. We spent several hours in Chicago, IL.

Merlene and I sat in our berth or the observation car during the day looking out at the ranches, and prairies where huge freshly cut rolls of hay dotted the fields. Cattle and horses, sheep and goats and a few wild animals roamed lazily grazing or just standing alone or in small groups. Lots of silos and heavy farm equipment stood near the train route.

We met lots of interesting people on the train. Meals were served in community style. We sat with different people at each meal, on purpose. We met a newlywed Amish couple on their honeymoon and a couple who had not ridden the train before. They were as wide-eyed and giddy as young children on Christmas morning. The food served on the train was good. We played scrabble and rummy all the way out and back to keep from boredom, and when we were not engaged with others.

We took a city tour in each of the three locations where we spent two days—Portland, OR, Seattle, WA, and Vancouver, BC. I found it interesting that in each city we began our tour in Chinatown, and ended in the ritzy residential part of town. In addition to the train ride out and back, other highlights included making comparisons of the three cities—how were they similar or different, and listening to the stories about the founding of the city. One of our mutual friends who live in Portland came over and had dinner with us on our last night there.

THREE WOOTEN SISTERS ON A TRIP OUT WEST
Tracy, California
(Levernia, Etta and Yvonne)

Three Wooten sisters on a trip out west.
Began their journey with lots of zest.
On Wednesday, September 5 at night.
They went to Baltimore to take their flight.
It was up, up, and away on a beautiful day.
There was sunshine all of the way.
Now, they arrived at the terminal right on time,
Claimed their bags, and waited for Gerald to arrive.

A very warm greeting was received at their new house.
It is very beautiful inside and out.
Little Miss Tiffani was fast asleep,
But Wanda was waiting up to give them something to eat.
It wasn't long before they were snug in their beds.

Gerald and Wanda had briefed them about their place,
and the town. They left a car for them to get around.

The first thing on Thursday was breakfast.
You see, they needed to be fortified for the rest of the day.
It wasn't long before they were off to the town.
They needed to mail their cards, see the sights, buy groceries,
and explore the grounds.
The town is small, so they couldn't get lost.
They found everything they needed.
They went back "home" and cooked a big country meal—
Pork chops, fried corn, cabbage, cornbread, and peach pie.

Now the restless sister was busy planning a tour.
She searched the AAA guide and scratched her head until she had it.
We'll take a Greyhound, and then a Gray Line Bus.
The other sisters agreed it's OK with us."

Friday morning after breaking the fast,
They rode the Greyhound two hours into
Union Station at last.

On a double-decker bus, they had front row seats upstairs.
They could see everything without any snares.
They rode across the Bay Bridge to Treasure Island—the first stop;
then on to Twin Peaks, all the way to the very top.
They saw many sights along the way—
City Hall, the Old Mission Delores.
They drove through Golden Gate Park where Japanese teas are served,
and took a shortstop.

The highlight of the trip was crossing the famous Golden Gate Bridge.
Then they rode through Fisherman's Warf,
and returned to Union Station again.
They rested on Saturday,
went shopping at the mall,
and went in and out of the model homes.
Wanda prepared dinner, and a friend came over —Gwen from Hayward.

Sunday was all set for a ride to Los Angeles via Riverbank
an out-of-the-way place.
They missed the first train which gave them a break.
They munched and munched all along.
It was late when they arrived a little jaded you see.
Amtrak sent them on a bus through the mountains to see.
After touching base with their friends and a cousin in another town,
they prepared to lay their bodies down.

They had an early breakfast on Monday.
Before the Guideline Tour took them across the city—
Hollywood via Wilshire Boulevard to movie stars homes,
The Chinese Theater, the Walk of Fame, the famous Rodeo shopping street,
and the Farmer's Market.

Now after a short rest, two of them went shopping nearby at the
Market Place and The Broadway Plaza.
Lots of shops and boutiques in and out.
The purchases were few,
but this they knew because the prices were very high.

Mr. Lowery picked them up at the Holiday Inn.
He took them across town to their little den

to have a drink of cool iced tea.
Ms. Lowery took them to Torrence
for dinner with Cousin Zoanne and Zandria.
"T'was a great ride out that night.
On their way back dessert was all they lacked,
So they went to the Hilton Gazebo Cafe' for a treat.
An early breakfast before checking out on Tuesday,
and then it was back to the station and to Tracy again.
Now they got in late, but Wanda had cooked, and they ate,
Rested a little before packing their grip.

Wednesday morning! Arise say goodbye,
and they are on their way one more time.
They must hurry, hurry with all of their might,
because they mustn't miss their flight.

'Twas a great little trip packed with incidents and events,
but the sisters had a ball,
and returned to Baltimore without a fall.

Carol and Juanita were waiting at the
Baltimore-Washington International Airport
to greet the sisters and take them home.
****
What a great trip out West!

VISITING ONE OF THE "A" PLACES WITH KAREN

On Sunday, July 1, 2007, Karen and I went on a 13 day trip to Alaska celebrating her 50th birthday. Our trip started from Baltimore/Washington International Airport, just one week after the family reunion.

The first half of the trip included land tours beginning in Fairbanks, AK. We visited some of the native areas, panned for gold, and rode the bus deep into Denali Park where we spotted many wild animals in their natural habitat. We took pictures galore. We sailed the second half on the Royal Caribbean through the Inner Straights from Seward, AK to Vancouver, BC. We had a balcony cabin, so we didn't miss anything. Although it was a bit cold, we wrapped up in our coat, hat, and gloves, took our binoculars and sat on the balcony to enjoy the beautiful sunsets and sunrises across the waters, and whatever else was moving. Also, we took side trips when we docked at three locations.

We flew over glaciers and went out into the waters where we spotted whales and seals and black bears, and bald eagles. What an exciting adventure. A little disappointed that no moose were spotted, but we'll get over it.

The ship had its own character—food around the clock, exciting entertainment, fabulous ice sculptures, and creative food displays, not to mention superb "dress up" dining each evening. We sat at a table for eight. Our table guests were very friendly, and our server was quite the entertainer which made for pleasant dining. And, there was shopping on and off the ship, and relaxing in the spa. There's no way to tell it all, so this gives just a flavor.

A WEEKEND GETAWAY WITH MY SISTER MARIE
September 2009

Everyone in my family knows it is a tough challenge to get my sister Marie out of Belgrade, to travel outside of North Carolina. She is a homebody if ever I saw one. I am just the opposite. Call me and say "let's" and I will say "go." I will stop whatever I am doing, and away we will go.

One day I had a hankering to "Get out of Dodge" for a weekend (so to speak). So, I called my sister Marie and asked her to "come on up and join me." Surprise! Surprise! She took me up on it. We planned a quick little family gathering with a potluck meal at niece and nephew Caretha and Clarence's house to welcome Marie, and as a little "send off" for the weekend. I invited my friend Toni Killings to join us on the trip to New York, and she agreed. I had already started making plans when Marie decided to come up— reservations for a place to stay, for the train, and a Broadway show while in New York. Everything was in place. Marie's son Averell Jamaal brought her to Maryland. Nephew Clennie Jr. transported us to and from the train in New Carrollton, MD.

As soon as we got settled on the train on Monday morning, Marie and I grabbed the scrabble board and headed for the dining car where we played all the way to New York. Once in New York, we got a taxi to the Bed and Breakfast where I had reservations. It was not ideal, but it served the purpose.

A great niece, Melanie Renee, who used to live in New York, came up from Washington, DC, on a bus to give us a quick little tour of some of the popular sites in Manhattan. We went to a show at a Broadway theater the next day, and had lunch with another great niece, Caletha who lives and works "across town." Of course, you can't go to New York without visiting the Empire State Building or shopping on Fifth Avenue and Macy's or milling around in Time Square. It was just a very short "change of scenes" to refresh and renew our minds.

On the way back, the train was very crowded. We were unable to play scrabble in the dining car, but lucky for us, we had front row seats. We stacked our suitcases, put the scrabble board on top and played all the way back. We became known as "The Scrabble Queens" in that short period of time. What fun and memorable time we had.

Marie actually stayed a week. We played lots of scrabble. Nephew and Niece Clennie & Barbara took us out for dinner at the Golden Bull one night.

The week went really fast. Karen and I took Marie to meet my brother-in-law in Virginia. It was about an 8-hour roundtrip, but I was happy to do that just to be able to spend quality time with my sister.

CONNECTING ACROSS GENERATIONS

Since I have maintained the same address for the last three years, I hardly know where to begin this little update. (Smile)

My calendar is always full. It is sometimes a challenge to maintain a balance of activities between church, Re-evaluation Counseling, hobbies, and the everyday mundane. Church activities include co-leading an anti-racism journey, volunteering in the office one day a week, serving on the Potomac Association Committee on Ministry, participating in a Life Review Group and a small group focused on Exploring the Sacred once each month. Re-Evaluation Counseling activities include leading a Black Women's Support Group monthly, participating in classes, workshops and leaders' meetings as well as one-on-one sessions. Pinochle is my favorite past time. I visit one of the senior centers to play triple deck as often as time permits. Also, I play single deck pinochle with some of my neighbors from time to time. I love making quilts. I haven't made one this year, but I have pulled out the fabric and may get started before the reunion. Now that spring is here, I get to plant and tend flowers in my balcony flower box. I also have a tomato plant in a big pot on the balcony. Last year I ate tomatoes from the plant in a pot.

Karen and I have been working diligently to automate our family genealogy. Actually, Karen has already automated everything from the records Sister Etta kept, and additions I have been keeping. We are searching on all sides—Wooten's, Holts and all other connections through marriage. So far we have traced the Holts back two generations from Mama (St. Annie)--her father, St. Mark and his siblings and his father, Isaac William. We've gone back two generations from Papa (Lewis). Genealogy is slow and tedious. One thing that makes it very hard is persons having the same name in several generations. For example, papa's father's name is Needham. One of Papa's brothers is named Needham, and my brother is named Needham. I believe my grandfather's father was also named Needham. The courthouse records do not always show jr., the 2nd, or 3rd, etc. Another case is the name, Robert. There are many Roberts on the Wooten side. It is hard to know what generation a given Robert fits.

It is great to be able to click one button on the computer and "spill out" all kinds of information on the family. This can only be done if the data is stored. Your help is sorely needed.

I enjoyed a week in Maysville during mid-May. I got to spend time with Yvette, play bid whist, visit a little, and just "hang out." I needed a change of pace and a change of scenery. I took the train which gave me an opportunity to "sit back, relax and leave the driving to them."

MY SURPRISE 50TH BIRTHDAY PARTY
1980

My friend, Toni Killings, planned an elaborate, fabulous 50th surprise birthday party for me. She left "no stones unturned" as the saying goes. Toni decorated the lower auditorium of our church (Lincoln Temple UCC) like a night club. She had a live combo playing music. A huge heart was part of the decorations, the tables were decked with tablecloths and candle lights—the works. She planned a "This is Your Life" program that included family and friends sharing significant things about phases of my life. She made a carrot cake that was shaped like the letters in my name.

My daughters (Karen and Greta) blindfolded me (Yvette was unable to be there), and told me they were taking me to dinner at a special place but did not want me to know where. They did not remove the blindfold until I was inside. I thought I was in a night club. When I entered the room, everyone stood up and shouted Happy Birthday! I was overwhelmed with surprise, joy, and elation.

That party was like pulling the ripcord on my parachute, or, you might say, launching my space ship. I have been in orbit and floating in an adventure wonderland, exploring my creativity, in many new ways every since. I have been following my own star and doing some of the things that make me happy. What a party! What an amazing breakthrough! What a friend!

PASSAGES
Age 65

Passing from adult into elder-hood was not easy for me. Facing the negative stereotypes of age 65 and beyond was depressing. I got caught up in listening to all the media advertisements promoting ways to stay young; noticing the magazines articles promoting products to cover your gray hair or erase wrinkles and other signs of aging. I even saw a hardcover book entitled, "How to Stop the Aging Process." I had a choice to make. I asked myself, "Do I buy into this mentality and become a victim of ageism, or do I take charge of my life and maintain my dignity and sanity?" I decided to take charge. I believe life is to be celebrated and revered. I refuse to buy into the notion that aches and pains are the results of old age. I believe that taking care of one's health and getting proper sleep and exercise will allow you to live long and be happy.

My niece, Barbara Davis, helped me plan an elaborate "Rites of Passage" party at the Civic Center in Trenton, NC. I decided to make a keepsake quilt representing the warmth and love of family and friends. I invited everyone to send me a square of fabric along with a note saying something about their relationship with me—where we met, or things they remembered about me. Making the quilt—putting the squares together helped me to recall and celebrate special times with each person. This is a gift that keeps on giving. My daughter Karen made a scrapbook with the notes and the description of the fabric. Having such a network of family and friends who care, gives me a boost whenever I review my scrapbook or wrap up in my quilt, or view the video of the celebration.

People came to the party from far and near. At the end of the "ceremony," I was initiated into elder-hood by one of my family members, who placed a stole on my shoulders embroidered with the words Elder. That ceremony and party pulled me completely out of near depression.

As we sang, "It is Better to Light Just One Little Candle," the overhead lights were turned out, and I lit one candle. Each person passed their light on to the next until the entire room was shining bright with candlelight. All praises to God for a fabulous celebration.

The week after the celebration, I spent a few days on Hilton Head Island, SC with my sister Marie and brother-in-law Lonell on the beach. It was serene and relaxing and helped me transition into elder-hood. Life is Good!

MY 75TH BIRTHDAY
FAIRFIELD HARBOUR, NEW BERN, NC
November 2005

My birthday celebration started on Wednesday night, November 9, when Karen took me out for dinner at The Market Inn, a famous seafood restaurant in southwest Washington, DC. She had packed her bag and brought it along so she could spend the night with me, and be ready to "roll" early the next morning. Greta came down from New Jersey early on Thursday morning. As soon as she arrived, we went to pick up the reserved rental vehicle. We placed our bags and other paraphernalia at the door. We simply transferred everything into the rented SUV and commenced on our trip to NC. The trip had been planned months in advance.

As soon as we were out-of-town, we started making our menus and a shopping list of our favorite foods. We talked about movies we wanted to see and just brainstormed on many things all the way. We shared the driving and made several stops. There was no need to hurry. We kept in touch with Yvette and Marie in NC via cell phone. Marie had dinner ready and spread on the table for us when we arrived. We spent that night with her and Lonell. We played games as we waited for Yvette to come from work. She decided to spend the night at her place and pick up her things. She joined us for breakfast the next morning.

Yvette added her favorites to the menus and shopping list we had prepared. Then, we went shopping for the weekend. We ended up with way too much food. However, once we had unloaded our luggage, food and other "stuff," we all pitched in to prepare and cook. Some of the time all four of us were in the kitchen. Each of us had our own specialty. Yvette and I had even brought along our favorite pots and seasonings, even though we knew there would be pots available in the condo.

The weather was perfect, and the condo was just right—two levels, three baths a Jacuzzi, 2 porches (one screened in) overlooking a lake where ducks swam lazily. There was no hassle about who would occupy what space. After dinner, I headed for the Jacuzzi, Yvette "hit the floor" for a nap that would last until three a.m. Greta and Karen watched TV and a movie. Soon we were all "out" from exhaustion.

It was unbelievable how early we were all up and dressed the next morning. Since we knew the menu, each of us just pitched in to make breakfast. We went into town to pick up movies and other needed items (no food). When we returned, we had lunch, played games, and watched movies. All three daughters brought their camera's and took pictures throughout the weekend both inside and outside around the lake.

After we checked out on Sunday, we said our farewells and "hit the road" for home. Yvette went back to Black Swamp, and Karen, Greta and I took Hwy 70 headed for I-95 northbound. The weekend was easy. Everything was perfect. We stopped to JR's, an outlet store near I-95, and browsed for about an hour then headed for the "open road." We dropped Karen in Washington DC around 7:30 pm on Sunday night. Greta spent the night with me in MD. We returned the rental vehicle the next morning then she headed home to New Jersey.

It was a perfect weekend. Just what I wanted. Lots of laughter, bonding, and reminiscing.

REFLECTIONS ON MY 80TH BIRTHDAY CELEBRATION
November 13, 2010

Talk about a celebration, this was truly a celebration to remember. It was electrifying! The time was right, the decorations were beautiful. Each table was decorated with different color napkins and matching balloons. Purple was my color. Seated with me were two of my daughters, two grandsons, my sister, one of my sisters-in-law, and my two longtime friends. The large round table was symbolic of my journey. I have visited and lived many places, and now I am back home—full circle. The food was delicious—good soul food. My MC nephew kept the atmosphere light and funny. Mrs. Coleman, the soloist, was powerful. I chose just the right songs that said the right thing. Guests included lots of friends from out-of-town, the community, and church plus many, many nieces, nephews and cousins. The weather was just right. I can't think of anything I would have changed, except to have more friends and family including my third daughter, other grandchildren, and great-grandchildren. Everyone cheered as I was escorted into the room by two of my grandsons. I responded in kind.

When tributes were spoken, I was able to listen and hear one validation after another, and take it all in as truth. I didn't get nervous at all. They said some pretty awesome things, The good news is, I believed all of them. I have come a long way!

The front cover of the program had a picture of me as my college (A&T) homecoming queen. I needed to let go of old feelings of embarrassment about being voted queen. Until now, I never thought I deserved that honor, and always made excuses as to why I was chosen. Well, that's all behind me now. It is all "out in the open." Imagine if I could have fully appreciated it back then. At least, I do now.

I called for a healing service at the end, which was spectacular. My clergy friend from Louisiana facilitated. Two of my clergy nieces and all other clergies in the room gathered around me. One niece placed her hand on my head, and the other niece placed her hand on my stomach, and together they prayed until I felt healing in my stomach. I believe my stomach is healed, and I can now eat anything I want without worry of bloating or pain. I am already enjoying raw salads for the first time in years. Yum, Yum! It was an amazing experience. It was MY night, and I splurged. I had a good time. I was spontaneous.

Several days passed before I got a chance to really read all my cards and enjoy the messages (over 60 cards). People took special time to choose cards that said something just for me. I've made a banner to display the cards so I can enjoy them every day--all year long or as long as I want.

This celebration was two-fold—a celebration of my birthday, and a fundraiser. Both were hugely successful. Folk who were unable to attend the celebration, as well as those who came, gave generously to The Open Gate Senior Citizens Program where I am a contestant representing my church Myrtle Grove UCC raising money for the organization. I was declared the winner between five churches and was crowned queen. Hurrah! Eighty is a great age!

MY 84TH BIRTHDAY

Our mom will celebrate her 84th birthday on November 2, 2014.

As her gift, she has asked for an "E-WORD SHOWER." She describes it as being showered with words of encouragement, appreciation, and love. She is grateful for her health, a wonderful family, and so many great friends who care about her. This would be a beautiful way to cherish those relatis not asking for money—just words. WORDS ARE POWERFUL!!!

Daughter #1 – Yvette Williams
Daughter #2 – Karen D. Godbolt
Daughter #3 – Greta Stewart

You are a strong woman who has and is an inspiration to all the women who know you.
Happy Birthday!
Jacqulin Williams

Delilah you are as beautiful on the inside as you are on the outside.
A natural leader. A compassionate volunteer. A true friend. I miss you.

Love,
Sue Dollins

Delilah (Yvonne) and I met at a Southern Liberation RC Workshop in Nashville, TN in how many years ago? Definitely, it's been a "few!" We made a decision to become sisters at that workshop and were encouraged by Laura McCray, a wonderful elder who grew up at Tuskegee and who was one of the important matriarchs in my church. Delilah and I have kept in touch over the years, and one very special memory is the chance to attend her annual family reunion which was held in Washington DC that year. My family and I enjoyed getting to meet so many of Delilah's family members (quite a crowd!) and my son, who was very young at the time, especially loved the day we all spent at a water park. The evening banquet was such a lovely affair and I was so impressed with the many presentations made by various family members. (My own extended family reunions pale in comparison!)

The next time Delilah and I saw each other was at her 65th birthday party in NC — wow, almost 20 years ago! My, what a regal queen she was. The various rituals and tributes she planned for her siblings, children and grandchildren were a sight to behold. I especially remember the butterfly theme and her love of quilts. It was another grand celebration which I was privileged to be a part of. Our correspondence through later years has become less frequent, but we always are in touch on birthdays and at the end of each year.

I have always admired sister Delilah for her active lifestyle, her love of family, her commitment to working through emotional issues (RC) and her deep faith. She has been integrally involved in her church, which is something we share. I was a missionary to Japan for 4 years (just out of college) and later to Korea for 8 years. Now, in my retirement, I am very much involved in the ministries of my church -- especially to teenage girls from generational poverty and to our neighbors in the nearby public housing complex. Delilah's skills at organizing big events for her denomination (not to mention her family) are inspiring. I consider her a model for me in many ways -- one of which is not being afraid to pick up and move to the next most appropriate and appealing place—be it her old home place, or the seat of government (DC), or near one of her children. She is always able to build a meaningful life for herself and find important ways to be involved, wherever she is.

Delilah, I treasure who you are as a person and as my sister. On this occasion of your 84th birthday, I wish you good health in the coming years, and continued meaningful involvement in the world. May you have many more years to grace us with your presence, your love and the inspiration you are to all of us!

Much love,
Louise Morris

Hooray! Hooray! Happy 84th Birthday Wishes to a special Aunt. We are sending birthday wishes with a smile and giving thanks to God for you. Your love brings sunshine and warmth the whole year through. As you celebrate "kick up your heels" because you are walking in God's grace.

Auntie you are smart...wise, .loving and kind...confident...compassionate, and you embrace change even at 84. The Wooten Family is blessed to have you to love. Thank you for always being there for the "Lewis Wooten" Family. As we age through the years, we grow to understand the importance of knowing our family history. We thank you for sharing and documenting our legacy for the next generations.

May mercy, peace, and love be yours in abundance. Continue to do what you love and enjoy the little things in life. May God continue to "pour on the love" so it fills your life and "splashes" over on everyone around you.

We wish you many more birthdays and we love you,
Franklin & Shrone Wooten and Family

I am delighted to join the E-word Shower for Delilah's 84th birthday. There are so many ways in which our lives have touched each other. We have shared our journeys at Christ Congregational Church UCC in Silver Spring, MD. We have been part of the Central Atlantic Conference (CAC) Consultant Services Network. We have worked together to dismantle racism since the

1970's through the Black Women's Empowerment Program and the Anti-racism Journey at Christ Church in the 21st Century. We have both been involved with IMPACT Silver Spring. In all of this, Delilah has been persistent in her efforts to make the world a better place. In the anti-racism work she persisted in spite of "being sick and tired of being sick and tired" of the depths of racism and the need for her to keep on keeping on. We were able to learn much from each other. Delilah has taught me so much about myself as a person and as a white male, and I deeply value our friendship.

There are tales to tell in all these experiences. However, that would take a book. I recall how we worked together on the Black Women's Empowerment Program as an example of how to use who we were as instruments of change. Delilah, actually she was Yvonne then, had a vision of empowering Black women in the Central Atlantic Conference. Black women were always taking on supportive roles in the Black churches, but were seldom in leadership positions. This program was highly successful and catapulted Black women into leadership roles at all levels of the UCC. As a white guy with some connections (otherwise known as white privilege), I was able to support her by making available resources and by personally encouraging her to carry out her vision. I was deeply appreciative of the metaphor that was applied to me at the celebration of this program at its ending - I was seen as the white water boy bringing in the sustaining water for the football team on the field. I cherish that metaphor.

And of course she is most gracious as a person. When we visited her in North Carolina, she introduced us to her roots in North Carolina. There was never a time when she did not respond. Even when she became discouraged, we could work through our own relationship with each other. We have a lasting friendship.

I deeply value my friendship with Delilah. My life would have been much less rich without her presence. I wish for her continued health and a continued full life.

With much love,
Jim Henkelman-Bahn

Classy lady.

Love your sense of humor, straight forwardness, courageous, challenging, supportive, wise, lovely, good scrabble player, fun to be with.

Ahead of your time, colleague, friend
Jackie Bahn Henkelman

Dear Auntie,

May the Lord shower you with blessings of grace, mercy, peace, prosperity, protection, and divine health on this your 84th birthday.

You are a shining example and reflection of God's love. I am so blessed to be your niece. I will never forget how you made me feel some 30+ years ago when words that you said released me from low self-esteem that I had been carrying for 20 years. You accepted me, and that meant so much. You are loving, supportive and faithful.

Melba Newsome

What a wonderful opportunity to share some thoughts about a loving, long-time relationship of kindness, thoughtfulness, sisterhood and community. Delilah and I go back to when I knew her as Yvonne. It just goes to show you that it really doesn't matter what you are called, it is what who and what that person means to you.

From you, Delilah I have learned the meaning of thoughtfulness, support of others, treasuring loving memories, the joy of working together toward mutual goals, and enjoying the gift of age.

Two recent quotes I share:
Youth is grape juice...Age is Fine Wine.
Youth is a gift of nature...Age is a Work of Art.
We who have been gifted with many years of life are truly
Masterpieces and so are you!
May God bless you with good health and many loving years yet to be yours.
Erna Bryant

Dear Aunt Yvonne,

It is with great appreciation and joy that I wish you HAPPY 84th BIRTHDAY!! I hope this will be the happiest and blessed of all your birthdays and that the Lord will bless you to see many more. You have been a tremendous blessing to me and our family, and I pray that the Lord will continue to bless you and give you the unspoken desires of your heart!

There are so many words that describe you that I decided to use the letters of the alphabet to describe you. Following is a list of words from A to Z except for 'x.' I could not think of a word that begins with 'x' to use. However, the following list quickly comes to mind when I think of you: Adventuresome, beautiful, caregiver, diligent, energetic, fun, giver, honorable, intelligent, joyful, kind, loving, motivated, neighborly, organized, pioneer, quilter, risk-taker, servant, talented, traveler, understanding, victorious, traveler, young at heart, and zealous!

You truly have a servant's heart and have given your time, your talents and your treasures and served our family and others in so many ways throughout the years. Only the Lord can repay you, and I pray that He will in a bountiful way. Your life truly reflects the virtuous woman described in Proverbs 31! Numbers 6:24 - 26.
Love and Thanks,
Annette Taylor

It is a pleasure to join in the celebration of your birthday. I wish you the you happiest of birthdays. I love and admire you, and have since the time I first met you. You are an articulate lady of beauty and grace. I am lucky to know you and am blessed to hold as my friend. God bless you and Happy 84th Birthday, and many more to come
Karen Johnson

Your Mom is wonderful. "Your kind words...." are heartfelt and her looks are stunning. If you said she was going on 80 or younger I'd be surprised from her appearance and manner. I'm so happy she's back in Philly. The photos are great............. but consider the subject.

Thank you very much for including me in the celebration. Warm regards,

Jim Dyer

Darling Delilah, I have a picture in my mind of you and Inge - the youngest and the oldest elder at Black Elders, and I see you standing tall, proud, full of excitement, and revealing in the moment. Your face radiated zest and gave us a glimpse of what is possible for all of us. I love that you are in my world and when I get in a tight spot I say, "What would Delilah do?" Much love and wishes on your 84th Birthday. Big hugs

Donna Paris

Sending you much love. You are a magnificent model for living life fully with connection and style! See you at BLCD 2015

Olivia

Delilah, happy, happy, happy birthday, to you, to you, to you! I miss you sooooooo much! May you have love, peace and happiness and all your hearts desires!!! I think about you often. Let's co-council real soon. I've loved you lots..

Khandi Bourne-Frye

Delilah, my beloved, Blessed, Earthstrong. Even now I see you, a light to all of us modeling a love and excitement for life and living. Love you lots and loads and always.

Chantal

Darling, dearest Delilah,

Like the wind, you are all around me.
Like the thunder, your voice rings in my ear.
Like the waters of the ocean, your love surrounds.
That's how I remember you.
Happy birthday baby.

Barbara Love

Happy Birthday Delilah!! Much love, and I am so glad you were born!!

Maxx

Happiest of birthdays to you. A birthday wish of full re-emergence. And many more.

Love ya,

Happy birthday to you awesome lady!!! I wish you continued happiness and much re-emergence. Hope to see and be with you next year at BLCD.

Peace and much love.
Robin

Happy Birthday to a phenomenal woman. Yvonne, during our 44 year friendship you have impressed me with your love of church and family. Thank you for encouraging me to join Toastmasters and for teaching me to crochet. Have a wonderful day.

Barbara Williams

Dear Delilah,
HAPPY BIRTHDAY!!! HAPPY 84th YEAR!!!!
BLESS YOUR HEART! I found strength in you. I have fond memories of us growing up as children in Black Swamp. Although you are older than I, you always had time for me. You didn't push me aside. You were a loving spirit, friendly, hard working and always had a good word to say. I am so glad I was your neighbor. I can't forget how you enriched Myrtle Grove even though your visit was short. (I miss you). You enriched us with the banners hanging so beautifully on the wall, your outreach program to keep in touch with friends and neighbors, and also pushing us to do better works. You stirred our hearts. KEEP STRONG!!! KEEP HEALTHY!!!! MISS YOU!!! LOVE YOU!!!

With Love,
Mahalie Harvey

Greetings, and the very best wishes for you 84th!!! Missed you at Church yesterday. Hope you were having fun. You are an inspiration to me and many others. Keep on Keeping On!!!

With Love,
Gerry Woodroff

To Dear Delilah,

As one of my newest and trusted friends at Old First Church, I send you love, good health, and God's blessing for your 84th! I cherish our getting to know each other this past year and learned so much about what you have brought to our UCC on all levels. I can't wait to read your memoir and all you have done in the name of Christ. The great and challenging endeavors you have been about over the years are revealed in not all that you say but the quiet deeds you have performed on behalf of God through His church. May God richly bless you with many more years in His service to humankind and all around you. Peace and blessings in the STRUGGLE which continues

Bob Polk

To Sister Yvonne,

I am so blessed that our paths crossed. Thank you for sharing some of your heart concerns and how you processed them. I reflect upon that wisdom when similar situations arise in my life, and smile because a MIGHTY WOMAN has shown me the way. Thank you for extending yourself to me.

Love you always,
Edwina Harris

Dearest Delilah,

Happy Birthday!!
What an amazing woman and role model you are in my life. When I think of you now in my mind's eye, I see a beautiful, strong African Queen. Your presence on this planet is such a beacon of light, creativity and determination. Your constant dedication to nurturing and healing yourself and our communities is an inspiration.

I see you wearing radiant colors, with poise and grace, tall and regal with those shining eyes and that gorgeous silver hair. I hear your voice speaking words of counsel and wisdom, poetry and truth. I feel your love and gratitude for the journey, even with all of its challenges.

You are a revolution embodied. A candle in the midsts, glowing with hope and heart and love.

I wish for you today, a magnificent celebration and recognition of the gift of your birth.

I am so grateful to be your friend. I am so glad you were born here among us on this Earth.

Warmest Heartfelt Blessings to you dear Delilah.

I love you,
Deb Tyler

Hello Delilah,

Older and bolder. That's what you are! I'm delighted to know you, and wish you the happiest day ever.

Much love to you on your 84th birthday!

Isheri Milan

I met Delilah at Old First, at the coffee hour after morning worship. Being new to the church is rather daunting and I was feeling a little nervous. She walked over to me and introduced herself. She then introduced me to her daughter, grandchildren, and other church members. She made me feel welcome at Old First. When I needed a ride, she was there for me. I always felt comfortable around her.

My description of Delilah is:
Beautiful-inside and out
Classy (clothes)
Intelligent

Kind
Caring
Happy birthday, Delilah. Have a blessed day.

Love,

Barbara Gurley

Friend, tall and straight, stately, elegant, faithful, supporter, puzzler, a world of life experiences we'd love to hear about. Just friends, but would like to claim as family-we'll settle for family of God. Keep on, keeping on! Many more happy birthdays!

Ellie & Mark Steiner

Dear Aunt Yvonne:

It is difficult to explain how much you mean to me and to our family as a whole. You are the ultimate "matriarch!" I am so blessed to have married into a family with such a loving Aunt. From the first time I met you, you opened your arms of love and welcomed me in. As an "in-law" I know all too well that this is not always the case. You are inspiring and encouraging in so many ways. I pray that I will follow your legacy and "enjoy life to the fullest!" I want you to know that I truly appreciate the time that you took to allow me to interview you and to visit your home when I was completing my undergraduate work at Howard. So few of my fellow students had positive, senior role models from which to gain insight. You were awesome! I was so proud to share the results of that interview with the class, and of course…..I got an "A" on my project….thanks to you!

I remember well how much you always focused on the positive and how much you faced each day with a ray of hope and thankfulness. I love you very much and I am thankful to the Lord for blessing me with such a wonderful Aunt. Whenever you're in my "neck of the woods," please know that I would love to have you stop by and stay. My prayer is that God will bless you with many more I happy and healthy birthdays, and that He will continue to shower you with love and all the things that you hold dear.

Happy Birthday and many, many more! Love and Prayers
Blessen Franks

Blessed and happy 84th birthday to a beautiful and one-of-a- kind aunt!!! May the joy of the Lord continue to strengthen you and allow you to continue doing all the many, many things you love doing. Thank you for your kindness and your love and for being a remarkable inspiration for us all. God has blessed you!!!

Love and hugs :-)
Lorraine & Gerald McNair

Hi Auntie,

Thank you for being my wonderful aunt for almost 61 years. You have been a blessing in my life. Praying that God will bless you with more happy and healthy years.

Happy Birthday
Juanita Franks

There is no better way to describe getting to know Delilah than to use the word blessing in the most powerful sense of the word. We have come to know each other across so many of the forces that separate our world - age, background, distance - but who I am has already been formed and strengthened by her after only a year of our paths coming together. When I think about Delilah, I often think, "Wow, how lucky I am that someday I might be able to get to be 84 like she's 84." Happy Birthday, Delilah! You are evidence of God's work in the world."

Margaret Ernst

Hi Aunt Yvonne!

I thank God He has Blessed you to see your 84th birthday. I love you and I am glad to have you as my aunt. You are an inspiration because you love life. May you keep flying like the butterfly.

Love & prayers,
Gregory Franks

Delilah,

I have loved watching election results with you. We were on the phone, not in person!!!
You are like the energizer bunny at 84!!!!!!!! And unstoppable!
I cherish our long relationship. Do you remember the year of your teaching the RC class and me assisting you?

Do let me know when you will be in DC again.
I love you,
Sunni Morgan

Delilah—My Christian Friend,
Grace and peace be yours in abundance. I Peter 1:2
For your wisdom and understanding,
For your constant faith and trust—
For the million and one unselfish things you've done.
For all of these and so much more, this brings you a world of
Gratitude for everything you are
May you be surrounded today and always
By all those things that are special in life.
It has been a pleasure knowing and working with you
In many Christian endeavors.
May you have the wonderful day you deserve!
Juanita Boyd Cooper

Pretty woman wonder where my secret lies.
I'm not cute or built to suit a fashion model's size
But when I start to tell them,
They think I'm telling lies.
I say, It's in the reach of my arms
The span of my hips,
The stride of my step,
The curl of my lips.
I'm a woman
Phenomenally.
Phenomenal woman,
That's me.

I walk into a room
Just as cool as you please,
And to a man,
The fellows stand or
Fall down on their knees.
Then they swarm around me,
A hive of honey bees, I say,
It's the fire in my eyes'
And the flash of my teeth,
The swing in my waist,
And the joy in my feet.
I'm a woman
Phenomenally.
Pre-nominal woman,
That's me.

Sis Barbara Fergerson Karara

To Aunt Yvonne,

Thank you for being an inspiration to our family & always helping us to remember the importance of family getting together. I always enjoy seeing you, and you have such a sweet and graceful spirit ... when I see you it's like I see a piece of my grandmother, and that is very special to me... as I miss her very much. I pray you continue to enjoy every day and throughout the year...I hope you have a blessed birthday, and many more!

But He said to me, "My grace is sufficient for you, for my power is made perfect in weakness. Therefore, I will boast all the more gladly about my weaknesses, so that Christ's power may rest on me - 2 Corinthians 2:9.

Robin (Franks) Talbert & Family

Happy Birthday to you Aunt Delilah!!! Affectionately called Aunt Yvonne from me!

The memories I have growing up will always be cemented in my heart, because are so special. We have such a deep bond from all the time we spent together from children to adults. You are not just an Aunt, but a friend, who I could talk to about anything and receive the best advice and honest answer, best laughs, and just a shoulder to cry on when I needed to. You were there for Sugar, dad and all of us, and I will be forever grateful. You were not just Sugar's sister, but her best friend, and you made her HAPPY and you made her smile. Thank you so much!

Your birthday! A time to celebrate God's creation of you, a precious diamond in life. A birthday wish to you!

May the sun rise up early to kiss you awake.
May the memories be gentle on your mind.
May the candles glow softly on your cake,
May your wishes flow warmly through your day,
May your prayers be answered with the light of God surrounding you,
Not just on your birthday but for all days to come.
Let the beauty of your smile and the love you give others be returned to you always
For you give of yourself from the heart.
May God continue to keep you healthy and grant you much peace and blessings
We love you and thank God for you in our lives!

Love! Hugs! Kisses,

Yes they are beautiful.
Rhonda, Harold, Michael, & Kristina

Dear Aunt Yvonne,

I want to wish you a very happy birthday. What a blessing to live for 84 years. I am truly grateful to have you as an Aunt. I wanted to thank you for making a dream of mine come true. After my mother passed, I truly missed her & I was sad because she was never able to complete her quilt. I want to thank you so much for completing the quilt. My sister and brother also share the same sentiment. My son has fallen in love with the quilt and sleeps with it all the time. It allows him a chance to connect with his grandmother. We plan pass the quilt around to each person in the family when ever a *new child is born.*

Once again you are truly a gem. Always full or energy and adventure. I have always known you to be my traveling Aunt. God bless you and enjoy your special day

Love,
Cryrstal Iboteh & the Iboteh Family

Hi Mom,

I just want to let you know that you have been there for me from day one (no pun intended!)

You brought me through all my ups and downs. I would not have known that I could draw and paint if it wasn't for the constant support through encouragement, buying me paint by number sets, paints, entering me in the draw sparky in the newspaper, taking me to arts and crafts class, and even putting my cartoons on your wall at work and in the reunion book. It was a tremendous catapult to my artistic abilities. You would tell me I could do it even before I knew I could. You were my charcoal drawing model, sitting still all that time so that I could draw you. Your constructive insights were very valuable even though not always warmly received.

You firmly nudged me in the direction of keypunch school when I quit HS because I thought I knew best (which was 100% WRONG !!!!!) That keypunch course led me through many years, getting a job @ METRO at entry level keypunch up to acting shift supervisor.

Watching you as you took care of Grandma Annie with great patience and pain (watching her go through) but you never gave up. finding creative ways for her to do what she loved, quilting and involving her instead of letting her just waste away. Even when I was in my own circle of myself I could see and admire everything you did to take care of her. Also Uncle Clennie, and Aunt Etta Mae.

I am doing what I love doing today because of the encouragement, guidance and struggle you went thru with me. (JUDE 22-23) And of some have compassion, making a difference: And others save with fear, pulling them out of the fire; hating even the garment spotted by the flesh. That is you pulling me out of the fire!!!!

Keypunch experience got me the job at 3HC (Home Health and Hospice) as a scheduler and the desire to help elderly and sick people (INSPIRED BY YOU) got me in school for Nursing Assistance. You even surprised me by coming to my graduation.

All these things I am still using today. Every time I look at the Banners at church on the walls I see you and Your gifted eye to see the whole picture, even when Tina and I couldn't see it.

GOD BLESSED ME WITH YOU FOR A MOM AND I AM TRULY BLESSED!!!!!

(JUDE 24) Now unto him that is able to keep you from falling, and to present you faultless before the presence of his glory with exceeding joy, I LOVE YOU, MOM

LOVE,
Yvette

Delightful
Easy to love
Loving and compassionate
Inspirational
Loved by many
Always thinking of others
Honest and true

You are a
Vital part

Of many people's lives
No one can deny the you
Nurture all who spend time with others
Even God looks forward to seeing you rise everyday (smile)

With much love and respect for all that you are!

HAPPY BIRTHDAY
Stay high Butterfly
Shirley Junior

TO MY WONDERFUL MOTHER-IN-LAW ON HER 84TH BIRTHDAY
Time waits for no one. Never change. hope and pray to God that I can live as long as you have lived, and do as much as you have done, see as much as you have seen, and travel as much as you have done….and learn to love everyone.

I love you and wish you can experience many more birthdays.
Ricky Godbolt (Son-in-law)

OMG! OMG! It's Delilah Yvonne Marrow's birthday.
I am thankful to be your niece. You have supported me so many times. Especially when I was at my most vulnerable, during the time of the death of my grandparents. I remember the letters I could not understand because of the words you used, which you continued to use and told me to look up. You have been a part of my formation as a person and ongoing inspiration. I continue to be proud to be one of your G-RREAT (in my Tony the Tiger voice) nieces and hope your birthday showers you with the love you have poured out on so many. I LOVE YOU! And HAPPY BIRTHDAY! E.Y. Frank, Inc. (Elizabeth Yvonne Frank, Inc. born Oct 13, 2014)

Martha Lewise Brown

Grandma,
Your life is like the butterfly you identify yourself with. Beautiful and flying freely. You are the model woman to emulate and your footsteps in our lives are one that I can only hope to follow and display in my children's lives. I love you and miss you. Have a blessed birthday!!!

Love Always,
Nacole

Dear Nana,

You are awesome. You are such a helpful person and everyone looks up to you for advice, words of encouragement and so much more. I can't wait to see you again and for Sunday dinners for which I love so much! Miss you!

Happy birthday!! I love you with all my heart. You are sweet and kind. Have a great birthday

Je'Vonte Smith (Great Grandson)

Lots of love and very good food on your very special day. HAPPY BIRTHDAY.

Roosevelt II

Hi there Grandma

Just wanted to say you have been a great blessing and inspiration through the years. I know as I have gotten older I've become a bit unattached, but I want you to know I love you very much. Have a great birthday and thank you for always being there for me.

I love you and HAPPY BIRTHDAY xoxo
With my very deepest love and affection,
Daryl Williams

Oh happy day, O happy day for on this day 84 short years ago God saw fit to breathe His breath into your lungs. I thank God for giving you to the world. So put down that umbrella Mama and let me shower you with love. Let me rain on you with words of pride, appreciation and admiration.

I am so proud to tell everyone that you are my mother. I appreciate everything you have done not only for me but for my children and I admire your strength, courage, and confidence. I have learned a lot more about you in the past year. I've always known you to be creative but I have seen first-hand how your mental juices start flowing and before long you have produced something fabulous and awesome.

You are self-motivated. I watched as you have been instrumental in getting several projects started at church. It's awesome the way people gravitate to you and want to be around you and want to hear what you have to say. They want your opinion and find so much value in what you say and do in and for the church especially.

I keep finding so many parallels in our lives. Since I have become a mother, I have tried to mimic many of the ideals and morals you taught or showed me as I grew up and I often find myself comparing them. I also find myself falling short but I'm okay with that because I'm not you and I know that you wouldn't want me to try to be. You lift me up when I'm down and always try to encourage me and the children to be the best they can be, for this I am forever grateful.

You are God-fearing. You follow the rules and set and exemplary model for what a Christian should do and how one should behave. I tell people all the time, I want to be like my Mom when I grow up. I'm still growing (hopefully, not out anymore lol) and I still want to be like you because you are the bestest mother, Christian, woman, and friend anyone could ever ask for and I am so happy that I can tell you this at a time that you are able to see it and read it with your own eyes. Here are your flowers mother enjoy them all, because after the rain of words there should be bouquets of flowers.

With my deepest love and affection,

Greta Stewart (Daughter #3)

THE SPLENDOR & MAJESTY OF MY MOM

I am blessed! For 57 of your 84 years, you have been my mother. So first and foremost, the blessing is mine for having you as my mother! I am thankful to God for blessing His child with 84 years.

> I lift up my eyes to the hills
> where does my help come from?
> My help comes from the LORD,
> the Maker of heaven and earth,

Psalm 121:1-2

You are the ultimate majesty of inspiration, vibrancy and truth. You are so deserving of those e-word showers of praise. Your essence and energy are characteristics of your symbolic butterfly. Your deep faith and ministry, your endless compassion for others, and your caregiving are simply you!

I could go on and on describing your love and devotion. There is no surprise that these e-word showers are testaments from your adoring family and friends. I know that your inspiration and legendary qualities of wisdom, courage, creativity, innovation, leadership and love will continue indefinitely. We rely on it!

You are joyful and full of life. You are the embodiment of your mother….one of the highest compliments I can bestow. All of her gifts have been consolidated in you, and you have in turn shared them with so many of us; particularly your children.

I credit you for sharing several of your attributes and being a catalyst. I got these traits directly from you -- organizational skills, having an eye for decorating/rearranging, photography (although you also videotaped), a passion for family & genealogy, writing & editing, church involvement, leadership, and especially your advocacy and caregiving for those who are sick, hurting or in compromising healthcare situations. These were, without a doubt, learned from you….and I am so thankful! They have propelled me in many ways.

It doesn't stop there however. Being "quilted together with love" allows you to connect with EVERY ONE you interact with. I know of no one who can honestly say they have not been positively affected by YOU in one way or many. It's simply not possible. Your love flows through your veins with such a passion that you are magnetic. People are drawn to you and then stick to you like velcro. You encourage people not only through your words but through your actions. You have a subtle way of nudging with the right intensity to make you feel like it is okay to go further and do better.

Ricky always loved and respected you from the beginning. After some initial resistance, you eventually opened your heart and loved and accepted him as your son-in-law. He will do anything for you and holds you in the highest regard. He always admired you and said, "your mother is so smart. I like being around her because I always learn something."

I appreciate all the times I get to spend together with you. I call you my "road dawg" because I wanted you to accompany me whenever the opportunity presented itself to experience life while traveling. We had a blast in Alaska and Africa!

I appreciate you for all your love and support through the "troubles" I've encountered in my past and the rescue missions you have launched and executed on my behalf. That's you….to the rescue! You were simply THERE whenever I needed you, and whenever anybody (in your immediate family, extended family or friend) has been in need. You have "been there" when you weren't expected. And, it was the "best surprise" to see you and know that you cared, you supported, you loved, you knew…..and, just because you are a beacon of light and a shining example of Christian love. You are what a mother, aunt, sister, grandma, nana, friend and cousin should be like. The best part is that <u>you are my mother</u>, and I am so overjoyed to wish you a

Happy 84th Birthday today.
This is the day the LORD has made; we will rejoice and be glad in it. Psalm 118:24

With Endless Love!!

Karen D. Godbolt (Daughter #2)

Your mother was stylist. She was a model in her own right. She probably doesn't think so, but in a different day, she would have made a perfect runway model.

Caretha Crawford

Hello My Sister Friend!

I hope all is well. On your special day, I wish you many moments of LOL joy doing and being what you enjoy most!

Best,
Mary McCurty

Hi Delilah!

I missed the community messages... But want to send a personal one to say happy, happy birthday! You are an amazing woman and an amazing gift to the world. Thanks for being born. I would love to hear more of your powerful poetry sometime.

Right now I am in grad school, so slightly less poetry and slightly more papers. I am enjoying it!

Love,
Erin

Delilah,
Today is your birthday and I wish you all the joy and happiness that this day can bring. I wish it for you because you have brought so much joy and happiness into the life of others. If I had kept up with my e-mail I would have responded in time to have this read at the celebration for you today. However, as usual, I am breathing hard to keep up with all the tasks in my to do folder. I do give thanks for having you in my life. Our journey goes back a great distance.

When I started out as a Christian Educator you provided a home for me at Lincoln Temple. I celebrate the times I spent at your home and the support you provided for me in the early years of my ministry. It was my growing years and having a friend and a church to receive me meant so much.

In my retirement, you are a part of my home in that your quilt is a part of the space that I return to for rest and restoration. The fact that you put your spirit in the making of the quilt means that your love and creativity is a part of the place that I call home.
I further celebrate that we now in our senior years have the opportunity to work together on a project that we both hold dear- Franklinton Center. Thank you for saying yes to the Council of Elders and for bringing members of your church to this sacred place.

I pray God continues His blessings upon you in your 84th year and know and believe that wherever the will of God takes you- the grace of God will always be around you to keep you in love and peace.

Much love,
Rev. Yvonne V. Delk

Hi, Delilah
Happy Birthday! No, get well first, and then have a happy birthday (observed)!! I hope all is well with the surgery and that you are taking care to let others take care of you. Why do I think that might be a challenge for you?! We spoke of you fondly yesterday, and want you to know how many prayers and good wishes go out to you today.

Love,
Margaret Rhody

My Dearest Delilah,
I am so happy you were born, and that you are a part of my life.
I love you, I admire your spirit, I love your connection to me. I love how vibrant you are, and how you keep reaching for your re-emergence. I want to be just like you when I grow up. I wish you all the happiness and joy you deserve on this great day that you were born.
I can't wait to see you at BLCD next year or at some other upcoming workshop.

Again, Happy Birthday!
With all my love,
Eunice Torres

Delilah, it was love at first sight with you, and increased every time we got together. You are a model of a long distance runner, and of the "little engine that could." I have you in my heart and mind forever. Be well.

Happy, Happy Birthday
Love
Marilyn Banner

Dear Nana,

I know I'm not always nice, and if you're sugar, I'm spice. But, I want you to know I'm always going to be here for you. I'll listen to your stories, and listen to your adventures, but nothing beats just hanging out with you. You're loving and caring, but most of all you're daring that's why I love you so much. Sorry I don't show it, but I thought you should know it. I love you Nana. HAPPY BIRTHDAY WITH ALL MY HEART.

TO THE GREATEST NANA EVER!
HAPPY 84TH BIRTHDAY!
Gabrelle Stewart

Happy Eighty-fourth, Delilah!

Enlightened - Fabulous,
Intelligent - Oh so precious
Grace - Unique
Honorable - Terrific
Respected - You rock!

And loved and absolutely wonderful. Sending my love, best wishes, and blessings on your birthday!
Much, much love.
Marion Ouphonet

When I stop to count my blessings, you're always on my list of people who have meant a lot to me. You have a way of giving directly from the heart—with you, it seems to come so naturally.

Happy Birthday!
Blossom Gica

One of the good things about getting older is that we eventually learn what is important and brightens our lives, and what is of little concern—but no matter the wishes and dreams in our hearts, no matter the paths that we take, the best part is the people we care about most and the wonderful difference they make.

Doris & George Hill

Today we are celebrating you—an amazing woman with so much love to give. Hope you have and had as many blessings and butterfly gifts!! Much appreciation for you and your friendship

Pamela Anderson

Even when life gets so busy, you are still thought of every day with love because you are such a wonderful aunt.

Levi Wooten

Today is a very special day, so take some time and enjoy yourself. Celebrate today with family, friends and fun.

Happy Birthday!

Winslow Township Center

Whatever makes you happy, whatever makes you glad, Whatever makes the year ahead the best you've ever had. Whatever wishes fill your heart, that's what I am wishing too. Because today and every day, I want the best for you!

Hope you will enjoy your birthday.

Marie Mattocks

God bless you on this glorious day! You are a very special sister, and you will always be a part of the warmest thoughts and feelings kept so close in mind and heart.

Janie Wooten

I hope you have a blast on your birthday! We miss you at the Center, and hope to see you soon.

Betty McDaniel

Love you so much. HAPPY BIRTHDAY!

Kim Murphy

Hello Yvonne,

I know I missed your birthday, but I was thinking of you and wanted to send my greetings to you. I hope you had a great birthday and that you have many more. I deleted the email by accident and had to remember how to get the information.(smile). Keep in touch.

Dearest Delilah,

Happy Happy 84th Birthday! I love you. I am so glad that you were born, and that you are in my life now and forever. Can't wait to be with you again soon. Have a great day.

Dorann

My, My, My, Delilah
My roomie, mentor, confidant, and Lady of Grace.
Happy Happy Birthday.

Love you,
Martina

Happy Birthday my dear sweet friend. I am celebrating with you the amazing miracle that I get to have you in my life! I love you.

Dorothy Marcy

PHENOMINAL NANA

Pretty woman wonder where my secret lies.
I am beautiful and built to fit a fashion models size
But when I start to tell them,
They think I'm telling lies.
I say,
It's in the reach of my arms
The span of my hips,
The stride of my step,
That's why I am a queen,
Miss North Carolina A & T
I'm Nana
Phenomenally.
Phenomenal Nana,
That's me.

I walk into a room
Just as cool as you please,
With a glowing halo,
With the kindliness heart you've ever seen.
Everyone stands and gives their applause.
Then they swarm around me,
Like a hive of honey bees,

I say,
It's the fire in my eyes'
And the flash of my teeth,
The wisdom, prayers,
And the joy in my feet.
I'm Nana,
Phenomenally.
Prenominal Nana,
That's me.

People themselves have wondered
What see in me

They try so much
But they can't touch
My inner mystery
When I show them, it's the God in me
I say,
The sun of my smile,
The love in my heart,
The grace of my style,
The confidence in my walk,
I'm Nana
Phenomenally.
Prenominal Nana,
That's me.

Now you understand
Just why my head's not bowed.
I don't shout or jumb about
Or have to talk real loud.
When you see me passing
It ought to make you proud.
I say,
It's the click in my heels,
The curls in my hair,
The palm of my hand,
The need of my care,
Because I;m Nana
. Phenomenally.
Prenominal Nana,
That's me.

Happy Birthday Nana! We love you,
Bill, Davida, Bria & Einstein

Courtesy of Maya Angelou

To My Fabulous Aunt at 84

Yvonne, you are one of the women that I have
Admired most of my life.
I still have visions of you walking
In situations when you were a young
Woman and I was a small child. You
always carried yourself with such poise and grace.
It didn't matter what you wore, you looked
Stunning. Your college mates were right,
You are a beautiful butterfly.

I can't believe how the years have passed.
Even though you faced many challenges, they
Only made you stronger, wiser, more powerful,
Determined, intelligent, and discerning.

God has certainly been good to you. At 84 you
Are still independent and full of life. Your
Creative abilities are still flourishing and you
Light up a room wherever you go.

Thanks for being that loving example of a
Vibrant senior…one who is loving life even
During her golden years.

Aunt Yvonne, you are my shero!
Continue to enjoy every day that God sends
Your way.

Love
Caretha

Dearest Delilah,
Happy Birthday! Where are you? Miss you much.

With Love,
Dreama

Dear Delilah,
Thinking of you with all the love and tenderness a woman can muster.
Happy Birthday dear woman. I look forward to seeing you soon.

I miss you and can't wait for you to pick a time when we can session together.
HAPPY BIRTHDAY MY BELOVED, DELILAH!!!!

Patience

Dearest Delilah,
Happy, Happy 84th Birthday! I love you. I am so glad that you were born, and that you are in my life now and forever. Can't wait to be with you again soon. Have a great day.

Dorann

My, My, My Delilah
My roomie, mentor, confidant, and Lady of Grace.
Happy, Happy Birthday.

Love you,
Martina

My Dearest Delilah,
Honey! What in the world are you doing for yourself? Taking youth pills? When I saw
Those photos of you, at first I thought it was Lena Horne. You are so beautiful in your old age. Ha, ha, ha! I miss you so much. I can think of so many nice things you did for me, but I can't write them all. Just know I still love you. You were my Oaks daughter. I will call you soon.

Pauline

Dear Yvonne,
What a wonderful way to celebrate your 84th birthday!! You have always been unique in your planning and executing special activities, and special days. This is another exciting, joyous occasion, in which many friends, and relatives can enjoy with you. My memories are numerous especially the time I spent with you at your home in North Carolina, and our trip to California.

Love, Peace and Joy,
Enjoy your Day!
Vivian Adams

I received lots of beautiful cards from friends and relatives.

SURPRISE 85TH BIRTHDAY WEEKEND

When Karen asked me to hold the dates November 6-9, 2015, for my 85th birthday celebration, I had no idea what she/they were "cooking up." Little did I know, she and her sisters were planning a grand surprise in Williamsburg, VA, at the Powhatan Resort—two levels fully equipped with two bedrooms on each floor and all the other space that goes with "time share" resort housing. I knew nothing. I didn't try to snoop—that would have ruined everything. It was a mini family reunion.

Greta picked up Mark from school in Seton Hall, NJ. She stopped home to pick up Gabrielle and me and headed south. When we didn't stop in Washington, DC, I was stumped. "Where are we going?" I thought. Finally, when Greta turned off Hwy 95, I started noticing the road signs. It was late, and the traffic was heavy. I still did not know.

The accommodations were fabulous, but I was thinking, "Why did they have to travel so far. They could have gotten something closer home." My mind was ticking, and I began to get an inkling. "This is close to where Nacole lives, isn't it? I inquired." Karen left abruptly and said she would be back shortly. She stayed longer than I thought, but little did I know, she was going to show Yvette and her gang how to get to where we were. What a surprise! I cried. This is what I had hoped for, but did not know it was in the making.

The place was decorated beautifully with a huge birthday banner on the wall, and matching table decorations.

Yvette got busy frying "a boatload" of chicken wings. She brought greens and mac & cheese with her. We stayed up late playing games and eating and watching TV until 4:30 am.

Greta and Karen were on the Saturday morning breakfast detail. The menu included bacon, sausage, grits, biscuits, eggs with cheese and, orange juice, milk (with chocolate syrup of course), water and hot tea. Later on, we had chicken nuggets with potato wedges, spaghetti with meat sauce. Yum, yum! Eating was definitely a very big part of the weekend. Food was available all of the time.

Saturday afternoon, they rolled out a big table-size doodle paper where everyone drew or wrote a tribute to me. Later in the evening, they had planned presentations including a video slide show with me at various stages of my life. They presented gifts and tributes. Karen made a huge scrapbook with categorized photos of other family members and me—very nice. What a beautiful birthday cake. We had cake and ice cream after the serenade.

Nacole and Yvette made the Sunday morning breakfast, along with help from the rest. The menu was the same, plus pancakes.

After breakfast, another big surprise was presented—a letter from President Barack and First Lady Michelle Obama, and a little book with messages of love and appreciation from everyone.

We took lots of group photos, laughed a lot, and had a really good time together. After all the cleanup and hugs, and packing up the cars, and goodbye chatter, we headed home with very, very happy hearts. Who was there? Yvette, Roosevelt II, Nacole, Je'Vonte, Jozsua , Karen, Greta, Mark, Gabrielle, and me. We missed Ricky - he was working, and Marquis was too far away in college. I talked with both of them on the phone who each shared personal birthday wishes. Daryl was working.

THINGS THAT KEEP MY MIND AND BODY AGILE

I love, love, love to play table games, especially cards. When I am playing games, my mind is concentrating on the rules and strategies of the game, so I can have the most fun possible. I will stop almost any activity to play a game of pinochle. My daughter and I belong to a pinochle club. We play with the club nearly every month. Sometimes we will call together an impromptu game.

I absolutely lose sight of time and everything around me when I am putting together a jigsaw puzzle. The shapes and colors intrigue me, and I do not want to stop until I have finished the whole thing. Putting the right pieces together takes concentration. I have developed a little technique that works for me. When my daughter is available, she and I will work on a puzzle together. Once the puzzle is done, we just take a photo, then break up the project and put it back in the box. Sometimes we exchange with other puzzlers or give them away.

I always keep a crochet project handy. I cannot count all the projects I have made. When my children were young, I made a vest and matching skirt set for each of them. I made numerous vests for sale. I have made caps and afghans galore. I have made baby afghans and afghans for adults. I have made all types of color combinations, by request. I have made afghans and caps and slippers to sell as a fundraiser, and I make them for gifts. I have made doilies and placemats and tablecloths. I have made doll clothes for my granddaughter, and even a dog sweater. I usually keep a basket or bag of yarn near my recliner. I must count my stitches and concentrate on the pattern of the item I am working on so that my project is completed correctly. This is another way to keep my mind stimulated.

I have a network of friends, relatives, and acquaintances that I have known for years that I keep in touch with. I am connected with several groups including my church, pinochle club, exercise group, and the Senior Citizens club. There are a variety of trip options—short and long. The Seniors Club is a great place to meet people and enjoy stimulating conversation. There are a variety of options for activities all the time. I participate with the "lunch and a movie" group once a month. There is really no excuse for one to become bored.

Quilting is one of the most enjoyable, and relaxing activities that I do to keep my mind challenged. My mother was a quilter. Mama showed me how to make my first quilt when I was recuperating from an appendectomy at age 16. She gave me the tools—needle and thread, scraps of fabric, and scissors, and showed me what to do. I do not remember much more about quilting until I was married, raised my children, and was living alone. Mama made so, so many quilts. We used quilts on our beds to keep warm during the winter. Mama sold quilts and gave some away as gifts, and to help someone in need.

When I first started quilting, I used patterns from a book or a pattern that someone else created. After a while, I began to create my own designs which is much more gratifying.

I made a quilt of the United States requested by a friend. Once I finished making the quilt, she had each state embroidered with the number of Peacemakers who gave their lives in the Iraq War. That quilt was on display in the City Hall of Jacksonville, North Carolina for approximately six weeks.

Raffling quilts has been a good source of financial support to help me accomplish several goals. I raffled a quilt to help pay expenses for my trip to attend the closing of the Ecumenical Decade of Churches in Solidarity with Women in Harare, Zimbabwe, sponsored by the World Council of Churches (1999).

I raffled another quilt to pay tuition for a multi-cultural conference on eliminating racism, and another was raffled at one of our annual family reunions to help defray expenses. Still another I helped to make with a group of church women, and raffle to raise money for the church's Women's Fellowship Program.

So far, I have given each of my daughters, my grandchildren, and great-grandchildren one of my handmade quilts. I made a sample quilt of the Underground Railroad codes. I took scraps and other tools to one of our annual family reunions where several family members made squares. I took the squares home and finished them into a quilt. A couple of quilts were made using the theme of the family reunion. So you can see, I love quilting, and quilting is very relaxing.

My sisters Thelma and Levernia were quilters. My niece Carol was a quilter. Carol was the only one of her generation in our family who showed an interest in quilting. She was making a quilt just before she passed away. I finished that quilt for her children.

Quilting has been a very valuable resource over the years. Our ancestors who were enslaved used quilts to send messages that would help them escape bondage. Quilts are used as wall hangings, table runners, bags, vests, jackets, and to recognize "causes" such as the AIDS quilt that was circulated across the country.

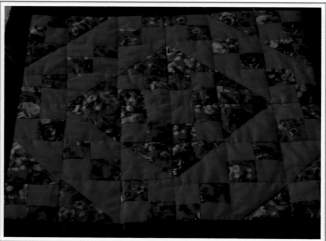

A PRAYER
1/29/86

Lord, I thank you for your love and trust in me.
Thank you for family and friends.
Thank you for insights and opportunities
Thank you for health and common senses. Amen!

EXCITEMENT
2/4/86

I can't sleep, I can't sleep, I am so excited!
There is so much waiting for me.
All I need is to be free.
I can't sleep, I can't sleep, I am so excited!

I have stayed in the Federal Government too long.
I have been locked and blocked and furlong.
Very soon I shall be free to create.
I can't sleep, I can't sleep, I am so excited!

DECIDING TO RETIRE
2/4/86

It has been so hard to contain myself since I decided to accept the offer to retire from the Federal Government. The world is waiting for me. I have been wasting my time and skills in this place. The time is just right. There is no fight. I can ease out without any hassle. Oh God, what a joy! O Boy, O Boy! I can hardly wait until tomorrow. There are so many things to do. I need to ready my space—a computer and a desk, and a hanging lamp − newsprint, and markers and paper and tapes--letters and phone calls to make. I'll be busy for days in all sorts of ways. UBC and Lincoln Temple and OCIS, CRJ and MATC, and my own little nest. My, my what a joy to behold. My story, my story will really unfold. I can hardly wait for the morning to break. My Lord, My God what a joy.

HATRED
2/1/83

I have a lot of anger inside me. I feel hostility toward all men. I become enraged when I think of all the years of mistreatment and abuse and the perpetuation of it still. I want to scream and bite and fight with sticks. I want to kill! I feel bitterness and hatred and poison and drums beating. I want to pull out hair and see blood running and bodies laying dead because I killed them. I see blood in my eyes and spit fire from my lips, and wear spurs on my shoes. I hate what has been done to me. You wretched souls of the devil. I despise the ground you walk on. I hate youuuuu! My guts churn, and my saliva boils, and my hair stands straight up while I rage through the streets with the roar of a fierce lion. Kill them! Kill them! The naked beast! Kill them! I must be careful of the innocent passerby or is there an innocent one. Murderer, slave master, beast. Take his head. Why do I suffer these angry feelings? I don't deserve any of this. Get off of me! Stay away from me! I'll chew you up and spit out your bones. I'll throw you overboard in the sea, and laugh as you drown. Let the lightning strike you dead, or a sword pierces your side. You are only pain to me. Pain, I tell you! When will the tables turn? Give me that whip. Let me crack it on their backs and watch them squirm. Pile one more stone if that be until it is impossible to carry, then demand that he walk. No water, parch the lips and tongue until he dries up from dehydration. Lock chains around his ankles. Make him walk in the burning coals. Roast his feet until they are raw and now make him carry that heavy load. Do you know how that feels my friend? You now have a taste of what I feel.

I am a woman! Look at me! Don't you ever mistreat me again. I am your mother, your sister, your aunt, your cousin. I am your niece, your child. Look at me! Don't ever turn away or fail to support me. I am powerful. I am loving. I am ME! GOD HELP ME!!!

4:25 A.M. – 2/1/83

I lay here in bed angry and frustrated because you are not here. I am angry because I want to place demands on you for which I have no right, and frustrated because I feel guilty about having these feelings. I love you, and I want you! I need you! How else can I say it? There must be a better way, and I have a plan. Will you think of one, too, and let's share.

It is truly difficult to be in this place. You must try to understand and help me. Please think clearly about alternative solutions to this situation. I've thought about it all night tonight, and many, many times before. There has got to be a better way. Sorry to lay this one on you so early, but we are in this together.

A MESSAGE TO MY SISTERS
2/1/83

Sisters, my sisters! Where are you, my friends? I need your support, and I need you to lend a hand as I struggle for independence. I have found one more piece of the puzzle in my life. I now understand why I don't want to be a wife. We've been treated so unfairly. There is no reason to stay there. We can, and must stand up all alone. We must prove to ourselves that we are very, very strong. We do need our men to encourage and support. We do not want him to smother us or even gloat. Help me to tell him what we want for us all. Help me to tell him it's OK if I fall. Just encourage me when I stumble. She wants to be taken care of, but from a distance, i.e. sit on the other side of the room, but don't get up and pick me up. In some ways, she is saying, "Please mommy/daddy I'd rather do it myself."

At this point in my life, I am wanting to explore my whole self—to experience complete freedom—to discover my full independence. How will I do this? First of all, I will discuss my feelings with my lover. I will experience feelings in my counseling sessions. I will accept a date with this man who wants to take me out. I will be totally clear with him and myself, about my needs in the relationship. I am no longer content to do things alone or with women only. I want the experience of wholeness and joy.

LONELL'S RETIREMENT SOLILOQUY

To retire, or not to retire
Whether 'tis nobler to stay on the present job, and make more money,
or retire and spend money already earned—stashed,
or make money another way.
I asked the opinion of others,
I stayed away from the job for a few days trying to feel
what it would be like to be in retirement.
To sleep and rest, and eat and rest, and ride around in my car,
and visit people whom I have neglected because of my schedule.
I could travel. I could start my own business—
Something I have always wanted to do.
If I stay on the job, I can pretty much do as I please.
I can catch up on the Barber Shop gossip.
I love to cut hair.

But wait, Catfish Lake Road is mine.
I have traveled that road for years—
in good times and bad—rain or shine.
I traveled that road when no one else dared.
Me and the animals are friends.
Why everyone and everything moves out of my way
when they hear me coming. They can hear me coming because usually,
I am moving at a pretty rapid speed.

If I retire, I will automatically become a member of the "Honey Do Club."
My wife will have a list of things for me to do every day,
Not to mention all the things needing to be done
that I could close my eyes and mind to if I continue to work.
I could soon get fed up with the "Honey Do" bit.
If I retire, I won't be able to pick up bargains
for my church and community, and home from the Base Exchange (BX).
As my late Aunt Nettie used to say, "I'm in a mess."

Then, one day I thought, enough of this indecision.
"Just do it," and I did it.
I signed my name on the dotted line,
So, on May 31, 1995, I walked away,
leaving the job and everything else up to God.
Now, I can gallivant with the other retirees, if I choose.
So far, this is the life!

FEELING GOOD

I am feeling good because I am in control of my life.
I decide what things I will do, and what places I will go.
My health is good, and the weather is beautiful
I am feeling good because people care about me, and they let me know it.

I am noticing the caring more and more each day.
Someone will call or write me a note.
Beautiful words are spoken on my behalf.
People do care about me, I know it.
I am feeling good.

I have been celebrating with friends I know.
We have enjoyed each other's company and that much I know.
I am feeling good, and that is the way it should be.
Feeling good!

LISTEN UP BLACK WOMEN

This is for Black women everywhere.
So you know they wouldn't know where to move,
If you put them suckers down.
Look at what we are doing?
We are riding all the suckers free,
And ain't getting nothing for you and me.
Take a look at this—
We are the cook, the maid, the nanny, and the lover.
We are the secretary, the administrative aide, and the deputy—
We are the queen, someone to look at,
and play with and shunt aside when we lose that glow.
We're the bride—a pretty thing for a day or so,
And then you know what happens.
We start having them babies and get to raise them, every one.
He ain't around two seconds. He is out having fun.
Look, sisters, we had better wake up, stand up, and kick them suckers off our backs.
Because if we don't who else will care. It's time, past time to stop this mess.
Yeah, I'm stopping the world 'cause you's getting off MY back.

KNOWLEDGE

What takes anxiety out and puts confidence in—KNOWLEDGE.
At the present time, I am very relaxed, feeling very confident,

And I am in control of my life.
I attribute this to the fact that I am in control of many situations in my life.
I have made a decision to do things my way,
And let others bear it or brush me aside.
If I am brushed
aside, I will deal with the situation then.
I want to keep this feeling, and I know the way to do it.
When I get frustrated, find a friend whom I trust, talk it over,
And by all means, keep thinking.

EVERYBODY IS GOING SOMEWHERE ALL OF THE TIME

Traffic was a bear getting through Center City Philadelphia at 4 o'clock.
It was "rush hour," and everyone was trying to go somewhere in a hurry.
I was taking my granddaughter to an Orthodontist appointment,
and wanted to get her there on time.
Some people are rushing, and they get mad when
the person ahead of them goes slow.
You have to keep your cool out there with all those big trucks.
You could get smashed or knocked off the road.
This ain't no time to get on the phone or lose your cool.
You have got to concentrate.

Everybody is trying to go somewhere all of the time.
You have got to stay focused, keep your mind on your destination.
Be prepared to stop, if you must.
I like to leave home in plenty of time, so I have no need to get stressed.
But try if you will, there is always a challenge to keep your cool and relax.
It is really okay if you are late for an appointment.
Safety is my goal, as well as being on time.
If I have to choose, I will take safety every time.

Wonder where so many people are rushing to—home, work, church,
the movie, the doctor, to visit a sick friend or relative in the hospital.
Why did they all choose the same time to be on the road?
They could ask me that same question.

At 85 and a half years old, I am glad to be among the crowd going somewhere.
I could be stuck in a bed, and immobile, going nowhere.
Going somewhere, just anywhere every day is a blessing.
I have got to keep my mind and body agile, be tough.
I am glad to be in the number going somewhere.

THE WEATHER

Kit's a tug of war between winter and spring.
Spring is bursting out all over.
The flowers are showing off their beautiful array of colors,
and the trees are budding.
The grass is a beautiful blanket of green, and the birds are singing.
Winter won't let go.
The chilly winter winds are still whipping around the corners,
And slapping faces in brisk surprise.

STOP THE WORLD

I'm stopping the world 'cause you are gittin off—that is,
I'm putting you down.
Do you know how long you have been riding free?
Why you brought me here from Africa,
And I bore all your children—
Black ones, white ones, red ones, yellow ones, too.
They have all been born by me.
Got some of every nationality riding on my back.
I have scrubbed the floors, washed the clothes,
Nursed and fed you, and even gave you my name.
What have you done for me?
You took me for a free ride.

You spat on me, sat on me, and put me on the street corner.
You kept me behind closed doors.
Yeah, you "took care of business matters"—
You kept me in the dark
While I was eating dirt,
'cause of the heavy load of you standing on my back.
You were rising to fame, and
When you didn't make it, who got the blame?
Yeah sucker, it is time for you to get-off-my-back!
I'm stopping the world,
'cause you are gittin off right now.
Git off Sucker!

WHAT MAKES ME BEAUTIFUL

I love effectively, i.e. care about people
I reach out when things are not going well,

As well as much when things are well,
I make decisions—take action
And spend my time in an effective way
To get many things done without taking too much time.
I am creative, natural, not anxious to go along with the majority.
I appreciate nature.

THE NEW YEAR

I saw 1980 slowly closing its doors last night.
There was nothing I could do.
I didn't even put up a fight.
I am ready to claim a new year.

Although 1980 was very dear,
I am so much wiser, and I enjoy life so much more.
One thing I have learned,
I can open any door,

My attitude for the New Year is to drop off the shackles.
Each new situation will be a challenge for me to tackle
I will sing a new song as I travel along,
And my days will be filled with love.

A SIGNIFICANT TURNING POINT IN HISTORY

Never in the history of this country has the atmosphere been
so charged with excitement, elation, and joy.

  We are experiencing one of the most significant turning points in the history of our country, indeed the world. On Tuesday, June 6, 2008, Barack Hussein Obama, a Black man, was declared the presumptive presidential nominee of a major political party (Democratic National). The whole world is charged. He is a great speaker, and his message resonates with so many people. He has energized so many new voters. While I am very excited, elated, full of joy, pride and truly hopeful, I am aware of the reality that not everyone sees the situation the same way as I do. The nation has much healing to do from the effects of racism, sexism, ageism, adultism, homophobia, xenophobia, poverty, hunger, homelessness, and so many other social ills that continue to plague the country and lay at the surface just waiting to leap out and overshadow everything that is good. Religion is one of the tools we use to help with the healing process. It is really important that we do not allow this momentum of change to wane.

  We, the Wooten Family, are blessed to be meeting in the Nation's Capital amid this excitement. We have a unique opportunity to strengthen the bonds of unity and cooperation we share. This is indeed a teachable moment.

Left: Caletha Crawford at a charity event with the future president; Right: Bryan Hager with the President.

DEFINING MOMENTS

- Joining Church and being baptized at age 13
- Voted College Queen (Miss A & T – 1951)
- Surprise honor by family at 10th Reunion
- Joining Re-Evaluation Counseling & 1st Black Liberation Workshop in Chicago
- Pregnancy and birth of my 3 children
- A training event in Atlanta, GA – "Talking Behind Your Back"
- Learning of my late husband's bi-sexuality
- Voted President of Black Women's Caucus, UBC/UCC
- Training simulating a 3-tier society
- Empowerment for Change
- Vandalism & burglary of my apartment and automobile in Philadelphia
- Moving to NJ to live with my youngest daughter
- Breaking my hip (fema) and recovery

CRITICAL CHOICES

- Accepting a Teaching Position in Armour, NC, after graduating from college
- To stay in a failed marriage for the sake of minor children
- To seek a divorce after 24+ years of marriage
- To move to NC after retirement from Federal Government
- Organize a huge party for my 65th birthday and making a keepsake quilt
- Travel to Zimbabwe and the preparation needed for the visit
- Move to Philadelphia
- Move to a Senior Citizen Housing Development
- Join Christ Congregational UCC
- Rejoining Old First CC in Philadelphia, PA

Dezein

Pivotal People

- My Mother
- Barbara Love
- Sunny Morgan
- Yvonne Delk
- Sister Etta
- Bess Howard
- Jim Henkelman-Bahn
- Ben Lewis
- Niece Annette
- Geneva Butz
- Nephew Clennie, Jr.
- Niece Caretha
- Pamela June Anderson
- Mereline Bagley
- Toni Killing

THE FLIGHT OF THE BUTTERFLY

1930 - I was born at home in Maysville, North Carolina in a little rural community called Black Swamp.

1948 - I graduated from high school in Jones County, Pollocksville, NC. I moved to Greensboro, NC to matriculate at North Carolina Agricultural & Technical College (NCA&T).

1951 - Went to live in the home of Rev. & Mrs. J. T. Stanley, in Greensboro, NC, to complete my senior year in college.

1952 - I was recruited to teach at Armour High School in Armour, N.C., and stayed in the home of one of the community residents near the school during the week. I hopped the bus to Maysville (home) on the weekends. I was employed there for three years, and was named "Teacher of the Year."

1954 - James Marrow and I got married, and I spent the summer at Ft. Campbell, KY, where he was stationed.

1955 - Got pregnant, resigned my job. Moved to Kentucky. My husband was deployed to Germany with Operation Gyroscope. Since I was too far pregnant to travel with him, I went to live with my sister Etta and her husband Clennie in Washington, DC, until our first daughter Cheryl Yvette was delivered on April 3, 1956, at Walter Reed Army Medical Center.

1956 - My daughter and I flew to Frankfort, Germany to joined my husband when she was six weeks old. He drove to Augsburg, Germany where we lived for three years.

1957 - Our second daughter, Karen Denise, was born in Augsburg on May 8, 1957.

1959 - Our family returned to the United States. My husband was assigned TDY at Ft. Slocum in New York. Me and the girls stayed in Washington, DC with my niece Barbara, whose husband, my nephew, was also away in the army.
When the TDY was complete, we moved to Ft. Benning in Columbus, GA.

NOTE: My sister Etta and I initiated our first family reunion that year before we moved. We stopped in NC, celebrated Karen's birthday, and enjoyed the reunion.

1960 - Our family moved to Baltimore, MD. My husband's next assignment was to teach ROTC at Morgan State College. Our third daughter, Greta Jeanne, was born August 12, 1960, at John Hopkins University Hospital in Baltimore, MD.

1962 - We moved to Fairmont Street in Washington, DC. We joined Lincoln Temple UCC. My husband was stationed at Ft. Belvoir, VA, where he was discharged April 5, 1963.

1965 - We moved to a larger house on Franklin Street in Washington, DC.

1970 - My sister Etta organized a 40th birthday party for me.

1974 - Moved to Greenwich Woods Apartment 21 in Silver Spring, MD.

1977 - Karen and I moved to Springhill Lake in Greenbelt, MD.

1978 - Our divorce was final in September 1978. Karen moved with a friend, and I
moved to Town Center apartments in Southwest Washington, DC.

1980 - My friend Toni Killings organized a huge surprise 50th birthday celebration
for me at Lincoln Temple UCC.

1983 - I moved within the same building when the management changed.

1985 - I moved from the Town Center apartments to buy a unit at Riverside
Condominiums.

1986 - I retired from the Federal Government in February 28, 1986.

1988 - After a couple of years working part-time, I decided to move back to NC,
where I grew up. My plan had been to restore the family house I grew up in, and convert
it to a small retreat center. I moved to New Bern, NC as a transitional year in
preparation for moving to the Black Swamp community in Maysville, NC.

1989 - I bought a new mobile home, and situated it right next to the old family
house. I cleaned up the yard, and planted grass and flowers.

1992 - When plans to restore the house "fell through," I moved from "down the
field" to the front of the property near the main road.

1996 - Went on a trip to the Middle East sponsored by Maple Springs Baptist
Bible College and Seminary. There were 19 on the trip including my niece
Caretha Crawford and my friend Merlene Bagley.

1997 - My sister Etta had a stroke in 1992. She needed "round the clock" care.
My nephew, her only child, asked me to be her caregiver until he was able to get
professional in-home care for her. I went back and forth periodically over a five year
period until my sister passed away in October 1997.
I stayed in her house for a few months until I decided "my next move."

1998 - I decided to move my residence from NC back to DC. I stayed in
Southwest Washington, DC.
Went on a trip to Zimbabwe, SA, as delegate to the World Council of Churches closing
of Churches in Solidarity with Women hospital.

1999 - An opportunity came knocking, so I moved to Philadelphia, PA, to accept a
part-time job at St. Joseph's Hospital where Greta received some of her
medical training. I moved to a large one bedroom apartment.

2000 - Went on a 17 day six city tour with 30 plus Howard University retirees
accompanied by my friend Merlene Bagley.

2001- Went on another train trip through the Pacific Northwest to Vancouver, CA.
I downsized to a studio apartment, which was also, in Philadelphia. That apartment
was vandalized. So, naturally I moved from that location. I moved to Cherryhill/
Blackwood, NJ, for one year. Each move was meant to be permanent, but turned out to
be transitional. I decided that I had had enough moving.

2003 - So, I moved to The Oaks, a retirement community located in Silver Spring,

MD, leaving my options open. I searched several places before making this choice. I wanted to be near one of my daughters, convenient to public transportation just in case I decided to stop driving or became unable to drive, and near my church home. I did not expect to settle down and say "this is where I will be for the rest of my life" until I simply did not have other choices. So far, so good.

2007 - Karen and I took a trip to Alaska to celebrate her 50th birthday.

2009 - My sister Marie and I went to New York for a brief "Get-away."

2009 - "Enough Already!" I moved back to North Carolina during the last week of December. I spent 2 1/2 months in Black Swamp while searching for just the right apartment in Jacksonville, NC.

2010 - Moved to Jacksonville, NC in March. While I believed this would be the place I would call home for a very long time, I was still leaving my options open.

2013 - Sure enough, "Here we go again." This time, I think this move to Sicklerville, NJ, to live with my youngest daughter Greta and her two children is probably not temporary. I suspect this butterfly has a new home!

ABOUT THE AUTHOR

Creativity and tenacity are seldom a silent duo. Nana, has continued to stand in defiance of injustice throughout her life, and remain an advocate for equality. As matriarch, she stands at the head of our family and leads us forward. Her children, grandchildren, and great-grandchildren look to her for guidance. She lives with my mother, uses her artistic and analytical gifts to assist friends and family with projects. She is always available to lend a "helping hand" if needed. As a young boy, and now as a young man, I have always experienced Nana as courageous, brave, and loving..

WRITTEN BY GRANDSON MARK STEWART

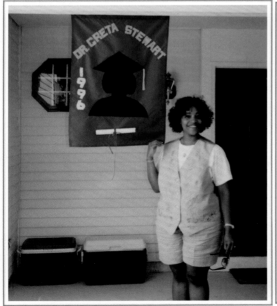

130

Picture and Image Credits

Cover - Flying butterflies flying among the branches - istock - Warawirl

Open book and feather (page 9) - istock

Pencils - Wavetop - October 10, 2018 - istock

Rosenwald School - Jumaydesigns - istock

Roses - AlexRaths - September 12, 2018 - istock

Flying Butterflies - Cheremuha - September 12, 2018 - istock

World Globe - vectorplusb - September 12, 2018

World Globe - Daria_Andrianova - September 12, 2018

President Barack Obama's 2009 Presidential Inauguration - Wikipedia

Flying Butterflies - Dezein - istock

Published in the USA

SoAllMayKnow
PUBLISHING

ISBN 978-0-578-56750-1